I KNEW HIS VOICE...

Listen for His Voice

Ed

John 10:27

I Knew His Voice...

by Ed Corbett

Pittsburgh: Serif Press
MMXV

CHAPTER ONE

February 5th, 1992 was a day that would change my life forever. Early that cold morning I saw love for the first time ever in my life. That Friday opened my eyes to the truth about what love really is. It all started about 5:45 a.m. with the words, "My stomach really hurts."

We were at a point in our first pregnancy when the baby could come at any time, so being a nervous first-time dad I called the local hospital on Camp Lester, Okinawa, Japan. When the OB nurse answered, I explained that my wife was having stomach pains. The nurse asked all the normal questions about frequency and intensity and told me that if she was going in to labor we probably had a lot of time. Nervous soon-to-be-dad that I was, I asked if I could bring her in to get checked out.

I figured the most likely outcome of the day would be hours sitting in the hospital—then we would go home with an all clear.

We left the house right before 6:00 a.m. and arrived at the swinging doors of the labor and delivery ward within 15 minutes. I rang the doorbell next to the door and sat down beside my wife, who at this time was in more pain..

The nurse came through the doors pretty quickly—a young Navy nurse dressed in hospital scrubs. As soon as she stepped through the doors and caught a glimpse of my wife, her expression changed. She was obviously paying a little more attention. She knelt and asked my wife a couple of questions, took her pulse and placed her hand on my wife's belly for a moment. She then stood, looked at me and declared, "Mr. Corbett, you're going to be a dad very soon."

We helped my wife into her assigned room and got her comfortable. The charge nurse told me to go finalize my wife's admission while they got everything set up. Since we had pre-registered, there wasn't much involved: just go down an elevator four floors, turn out of the elevator and into the admissions office, sign a paper and return.

I figured she was in good hands—and, besides, everything I had learned about labor told me that we had hours before the baby would come.

How wrong that assumption was! Within two minutes of my walking into the admissions office, the phone rang. The clerk on duty answered as I stepped up to the counter. "Yes...I think he just walked in...Will do, ma'am."

He hung up and looked up at me and said, "Are you Sgt. Corbett?"

"Yes."

"The charge nurse on the delivery floor said to get back up there in a hurry. Your wife is ready to deliver."

I hurried up the elevator and entered the delivery room. As I stepped through the door, a doctor turned to me and smiled. She looked over at my wife and said, "O.K., Mrs. Corbett, your husband is now here. Let's have this baby."

It was just a few pushes and a couple of those breathing exercises we had learned in class when we heard the doctor exclaim, "It's a beautiful little girl."

The nurses came over and took my new daughter from the doctor to a small table to examine her.

My head was spinning. This all was happening so fast, I couldn't even catch my breath. I figured I had a few minutes at least while they examined my new daughter, Kristina, so I stood beside my wife, holding her hand and helping comfort her after the whirlwind delivery. I kept looking at the nurses huddled around the little heating table, hoping everything was all right and just overcome with desire to see my Kristina.

The charge nurse looked over at the doctor and gave some vitals and statistics, then looked at me and asked if I wanted to see my baby girl. All I could think was how silly that question was. I had waited nine months to see this child. Of course I wanted to meet this precious baby!

I nervously approached the table she was on and took my first look at Kristina. My breath was stolen from me. I remember thinking before she was born how possessive fathers were with their little girls. I jokingly

called it the "Daddy Syndrome." You know it
—fathers are so protective of their daughters.
No man can ever be good enough, no dream
ever big enough, and no pain she feels small
enough to break your heart. Daddy's little girl
—his princess. I teased my friends with
daughters. She owns daddy's heart and has
him wrapped around her finger. I believed
that I would never be overprotective of any
daughter I would have.

Well, that all changed early that February
morning with that newborn little six-pound
Kristina. Too weak to even lift her head, she
opened those dark eyes and pulled me in. The
only thought I had was no one would ever be
worthy of this girl's heart.

Now, I hadn't prayed in a long time or really even thought about God in several years.
Though I had grown up Christian and was
raised Catholic, I hadn't ever made my faith
important in any way. But in that moment I
found myself thanking God for this angel
whom He had blessed me with. For the first
time in my life, as I gazed upon this little
baby, I knew what true love felt like. This precious girl had my heart with a simple glance.
It was truly love at first sight.

Even as Kristina grew through the years, she always owned my heart. As we anticipated the birth of our second daughter, Kaitlyn, the USAF transferred us from Okinawa, Japan, to Davis Monthan AFB in Tucson, AZ. I found myself wondering how I could possibly love anyone more than I loved Kristina. Then Kaitlyn was born, and somehow my knowledge and capacity for love grew incredibly. A couple years later, after being discharged from the USAF, our son, Christopher, was born and I found my love growing again. And in each of my children I always find myself thanking God for the incredible gifts with which He has blessed my life.

Not long after the birth of my son, I found myself in the middle of a divorce. I managed to maintain custody of my three children. They were all my life.

After a few years, life started to settle down and at the prompting of a friend I posted a dating ad on AOL, simply seeking companionship, not a relationship. But yet again, God surprised me, giving me incredible love out of the blue—this time with a woman straight from His hands. Not only was I blessed with a great woman of faith, but she brought with her a new daughter to add to my blessings. The day after our first date, our kids met and it was an instant bond.

Within a year of posting that dating ad, we were married. This woman opened my eyes to God's presence and through her example brought me back to a relationship with Christ. Before I met Connie I was a person who didn't have any idea of who God was, and within just a few years of marriage she helped me grow to know and want a relationship with Him.

Little did I know how much I would need that in the years to come.

C H A P T E R   T W O

Once Kristina went to Mass with her grandmother. When she came home, she said to me, "Daddy, did you know Jesus loves you? I know because He told me at church today." She had such pure and blind faith.

I chalked that up to what the priest must have said in him sermon...but later events have made me wonder about that.

As Kristina grew, one thing remained clear: She had a pure heart oriented toward God. As she turned fourteen, she started feeling a calling to give her life as a religious sister, and started looking at various religious orders. At seventeen she found a missionary order and invited a sister from the Missionary Sisters of the Holy Rosary visit our home. They spent hours together, and Kristina felt a strong pull toward their mission. She set herself to that goal. Kristina started college with the thought that she was going to be a religious sister when she graduated. As a religious sister she would need to enter an order free of debt, so she explored the possibilities of finishing school this way. She started working a full-time job at McDonald's while taking on a full class load at the nearby a community college. Though the schedule was rough, she was having the time of her life meeting new friends at school. Though just in her first semester, she already had the second semester paid for. To say that Kristina was having the time of her life is an understatement. She was attending school full time and adapting well to her life as a college freshman. She was learning and expanding her mind with every day. She was meeting new friends, hanging out in the student union, and just enjoying school. Work was forming her to be a trainer; she was the employee of the month and getting enough hours start paying for the third semester of school already.

Early November 2010 started well, but things changed with simple swollen feet and ankles.

When Kristina told us her feet and ankles were swollen, we just figured this was due to long hours standing and not enough time resting her legs. We told her to just keep an eye on them and elevate them on her days off. Things would be better in a couple of days.

Our son, Christopher, was confirmed on November 6th, 2010. The Bishop came to our church to confirm his class of more than 100 confirmation candidates. It was a great day for our parish and our family. Family came in from out of town to help us celebrate this great event. Before the service, our family sat together enjoying each other's company. As Kristina spoke with her grandmother and told her about her classes and how well things were going in school and at work, she mentioned her swollen feet and ankles. Her grandmother immediately was concerned, telling her she needed to go to the doctor as soon as she could to get them checked out. She was afraid because our family has a history of heart disease, and thought her swollen ankles might be a sign of heart problems. She made Kristina promise that she'd go get it checked out just to make sure.

The next morning, Kristina was off from work, so she decided that immediately following Sunday morning Mass she would go over to the urgent care and have her ankles checked out. We figured it wouldn't take that long for the doctors to determine that she was just spending a lot of time on her feet and nothing was really wrong. They give her our same recommendations: cut back a few hours at work and prop your feet until the swelling subsides.

A few hours later Kristina called and told us the doctors were getting ready to send her home and wanted her to follow up with her primary physician. They had run some labs and were concerned with the high amount of protein in her urine. The doctors weren't sure what the cause was but suggested she set the primary care follow-up as soon as possible. The doctor explained that protein is very important in your body as it helps the vascular system carry fluid from the cells throughout the body to the kidneys which then filters the fluid, sending the protein back through the body while expelling excess fluid from the body. In Kristina's case her kidneys were dumping that protein from her body, which then didn't leave enough within her to carry the fluid from the cells. That was what caused the swelling.

Kristina called her primary physician Monday morning and set up an appointment two days later. Her primary doctor repeated the same labs the urgent care had done just a few days earlier. The results came back and still showed very high levels of protein and trace blood in her urine. Her primary doctor recommended she follow-up immediately with a nephrologist—a doctor specializing in the kidneys.

We spent a day searching for local nephrologists in the area who also were accepting new patients. This wasn't an easy task. There were a lot of these specialists in the area, but many weren't accepting new patients or didn't have appointments available for several weeks. Kristina's primary doctor made it pretty clear that she wanted this follow-up as soon as possible. So we continued to search.

We finally found a doctor in nearby Washington, Pennsylvania, who could see her in about a week. The doctor took her back to the exam room and spent quite a while with her while I sat out in the waiting room. Kristina was 18, so she didn't need daddy tagging along for this. She could handle it. So I waited, reading outdated magazines and worrying about what was going to happen.

After what seemed like hours had passed, the door opened, and Kristina stepped out with a smile. I stood and greeted her and the doctor. Her doctor asked Kristina if she wanted him to speak to me about the examination. She was fine with that. So I followed them into the exam room. I stood as the doctor explained that Kristina was losing an extremely high amount of protein in her urine, and that there was also trace blood as well. He recommended that she have a kidney biopsy done as soon as it could be scheduled to figure out the reason for the protein loss. The doctor said he could see three different reasons for her kidneys to be dumping so much protein. The first and most likely was a condition called minimal change disorder, with the least likely, but most severe, possibility being lupus. While we were talking Kristina was setting up the appointment at the hospital for the kidney biopsy. The kidney biopsy was set for the day before Thanksgiving. The plan was that I would take the day off from work: we'd have the biopsy done in the morning and be home early enough for Kristina to rest from the procedure, and then head to Ohio to celebrate Thanksgiving with my wife's family, as has become our tradition. It would be a nice weekend with family away from everything.

The weekend lived up to all expectations.

The following week the nephrologist called our house. He said that the results of the biopsy weren't fully in yet, but that preliminary results reported a strong possibility of lupus—the disease he said was most severe but least likely not long ago. We had heard of lupus before, but just in passing. We really knew nothing about the disease itself. He explained that lupus was an auto-immune disease and that basically her body was attacking her own kidneys. He said he wasn't extremely familiar with the condition either and would start doing some heavy research while we waiting for the full, finalized results to come back.

It only took a few more days to get the official diagnosis—lupus nephritis, a form of lupus affecting the kidneys. This is one of the most severe manifestations of the disease, which can result in renal failure and death.

C H A P T E R   T H R E E

Time was going crazy all of the sudden. We had been a calm, day-to-day, ordinary household with a college student, two high school seniors and a freshman. Now we felt as if we had totally lost control. I can remember that first night when we received the news of the official diagnoses and the fears that ran through my mind. The worst feeling in the world for a parent is to hear that your child is sick and there is nothing that you can do to make her better. I can remember crying out to God that night, "how could You do this to us? I've done so much for you and all I've ever asked is 'Thy will be done to me, but never touch my family, always keep them safe.' And You respond by doing this to Kristina? The young lady who wanted to give her life to Your service? I've been very active in our parish and in the Diocese of Pittsburgh. I've been running a men's fellowship group and Scripture study group at our church. I was active in a men's retreat group. Just a few months ago I led the spring Emmaus retreat for our area. Haven't I done enough to keep my family safe?"

On the trolley to work the following morning, as had become my practice of allowing God to speak to me, I placed my Bible on my lap and let it fall open to the pages God wanted me to read. This is part of a form of prayer called Lectio Divina, which was developed long ago by St. Benedict the Abbot. You pick a passage and read it, identifying a word or passage that stands out. Then you reflect on that passage and how it may play in your life. The idea is to listen for God to speak through His Holy Word.

That morning my Bible fell open to the Book of Job.

For the first several minutes I could only stare at the page. I couldn't even read any of the words. I knew the story of Job—God had given Satan permission to "attack" Job to prove that, when this man lost the blessings God had given him, he would turn his back on

God. God was confident that he would not. In the story Job lost just about everything he had, but tenaciously kept his faith. In the end he proved his faith was stronger than the things in his life.

I honestly have to say that, as I stared at that page, I was terrified. I knew I didn't have the faith of Job. I was afraid that, if put to the test, I would fail. I also feared losing the things most important to me the way Job had. I was afraid for my daughter. This girl taught me my first lesson of what unconditional love was and how great it was to give it.

In those couple of days waiting on the diagnosis to come back from pathology, her doctor had in fact done a lot of research and gave us a lot of information on the condition and the specific types that were affecting Kristina.

The biopsy came back positive. Kristina was diagnosed with lupus—the biopsy confirmed 25% damage to her kidney cells already. Because of the severity and risks of the form of lupus nephritis, her doctor recommended that Kristina immediately begin a high-dose steroid treatment, and that she go to the hospital for outpatient IV steroid treatments. These IV steroid treatments would dose her body with steroids to provide quick medicinal protection of her kidneys. The treatment would consist of three IV sessions at the hospital that would last a couple of hours each and shouldn't have many negative side effects to Kristina, except maybe a few hours of nausea. He put her on several other oral medications to start controlling and treating this disease.

The doctor also said the long-term treatment of this condition would be another IV drug known as Cytoxan. This is a strong chemotherapy drug, often used to treat cancers and leukemia but also used to treat lupus. The dosage given to lupus patients would be considerably lower than what is given to cancer patients. He spoke to Kristina in detail, explaining the risks and side-effects of the Cytoxan. One of the biggest concerns was the risk of infertility, especially since Kristina was just 18 years old. He told her that if she desired she could have eggs harvested as a precaution, so she could still have children in the future if the drug did make her infertile. She told him she needed to think about it first. He advised not to take too long because he wanted to start the treatment as quickly as possible. The egg harvesting would need to be done before the steroid IV could start, as the longer the delay, the higher the risk of further damage to her kidneys.

That evening my wife and I had friends visiting the house for a monthly couples' study group. We would meet to talk about specific readings from whatever book of the Bible we were studying. This group of close friends came together as much for the fellowship and friendship as the study.

One of our members is our previous pastor. He came to our first study to help us get started and continued to join us. Kristina was concerned about the Church's teachings and stance on harvesting eggs. She understood how precious life is to the Church. She didn't want to risk harming a child through the decision or possibly putting an unfertilized egg in harm. Father Sam gave Kristina some information on a Catholic organization on bioethics that could help her find the answer to her questions and concerns.

All of our friends that night expressed deep, heartfelt concern and made a point of praying for Kristina with us that evening and have continued to pray for her since.

The following morning Kristina worked early. About midday she called home wanting to talk about the treatment. She was overwhelmed and pretty scared. I asked if she had had a chance to call the number Father Sam had given us yet. She said she had thought about and prayed about it all morning and had decided she didn't want to wait to start her treatment. She decided that her kidneys are more important, and that if God wanted her to have children when she got older, she would, regardless of what medicines she may take now, not to mention that there are thousands of babies who would love to find a new mother. If she couldn't have her own children, she could adopt one of these. I was surprised, though I guess I shouldn't have been, that in this time of struggle and fear, Kristina was still thinking of someone else and held strongly to her faith that "with God all things are possible."

Her nephrologist in the meantime did some additional research and spoke to colleagues about lupus nephritis. He discovered a newer drug that had been finding success called CellCept. The advantage of this drug was that it didn't have the higher risks and side effects of the Cytoxan, mainly the infertility risk. The CellCept was taken orally in the form of a pill. Kristina would expect to be on this medicine for a few years at least, if it worked. The main advantage of the Cytoxan, though, was that it has a long track record combating lupus nephritis and has been highly successful, while the CellCept was just a lot newer. The doctors explained that different patients react differently to various medications. One medicine may work very well for one patient, but may not be as effective for another patient. And what didn't work for one patient may be very effective for another.

After some consultation with the doctor, it was decided to start the CellCept and give it three or four months to work. The benefits simply outweighed the risk for Kristina and the potential side effects. If the CellCept wasn't successfully treating her condition, we could always switch to the Cytoxan later.

CHAPTER FOUR

The following weekend the Diocese of Pittsburgh happened to have their annual teen retreat. This weekend has always been spectacular. Hundreds of teens come together on a rustic site for a weekend filled with praise, worship, fellowship, learning and a real opportunity to find Jesus Christ with their peers. I've attended this retreat as a volunteer for the past few years since Kristina was a freshman in high school and made her first trip there.

This was my first year attending without Kristina. But, since my two other daughters, Samantha and Kaitlyn, were there, I went again as a chaperone.

I always seem to get more from the teens than I give to them. Their clarity of vision always humbles me and teach me something I

couldn't have thought of otherwise. This year
we arrived early and were able to get the
teens checked in and settled into their cabins
quickly. I watched as the boys I was leading
drew together in the cabin with their music
and football. I could see the real excitement
and joy in their faces and in the tone of their
voices. I could never figure out where they
came up with such a seemingly endless sup-
ply of energy.

The first event of the weekend is always the
initial welcome in the Tab, short for tabernacle—the main room where most of the weekend would be spent. To enter the main room
of the Tab you go through a large set of glass
doors into a lobby: the Tab is located just in
front of you, with a small makeshift chapel always located in a small and private room to
the left.. Throughout the retreat weekend, the
Blessed Sacrament, our Lord Jesus Christ, is
always set up in this small chapel for perpetual adoration and prayer throughout the
weekend.

This weekend was no different. A small
sign hung on the door asking silence around
this area so those within might have a peaceful and quiet time. Adult chaperones are

asked to pray for the teens sometime throughout the weekend. Although the teens always
abound in that perpetual energy and never
seem to settle enough to sleep, it isn't un-
usual to find 3-4 adults in the room at all
hours of the day and night lost in prayer. As I
entered this lobby area I felt a tug to go to
pray in the chapel. It was almost like I heard
Him calling for me to come sit with Him. I
even felt a strange tugging, seeming to pull
me gently toward the door. Being the first
event of the weekend, the welcome was always energetic and exciting. Another part,
important for adults was the chaperone meeting to describe our duties and responsibilities
for the weekend. So, I resisted the pull, decid-
ing I would go later when things were calmer
and I had more time. Yet, while sitting in the
meetings I kept thinking of our Lord calling
to me to join Him.

Following our adult meeting we rejoined
the teens and had a short period of praise
songs and prayer. It is always so uplifting to
see several hundred teens from around the
Pittsburgh area lifting the arms and voices to
praise our Lord. There is nothing like seeing
teens dancing for joy, some of the teens openly

praising for the first time. Immediately following this we were ushered to the cafeteria for a late-night treat, remarkable pizzas made on-site by other adult volunteers serving in the kitchen. But as I headed for cafeteria doors I again felt that pull toward the adoration chapel and that voice beckoning me, "Come here."

I glanced at the front door and the exiting teens, then turned right and quietly opened the chapel door. I entered, taking an open place to the right side, and got on my knees before our Lord present in His Blessed Sacrament. Crossing myself in the name of the Father, Son and Holy Spirit I bowed my head and began to pray. Then, strangely, each of the other people praying in the room one by one stood and left the room. Within minutes of entering I found myself alone in the room, just my God and I in a quiet, candlelit room.

As I gazed upon our Lord in the Blessed Sacrament I started my prayers with the prayer He taught us: "Our Father, who art in Heaven..." As I finished, my prayer shifted quickly to my present need and quickly my fears immediately starting spilling out in my prayer. "Father, how could you allow this to happen to my daughter? We love you; where are you?" The past few days I had almost had a sense of abandonment of God. I couldn't stop wondering if God loved us even just as much as we believed that He did. If He truly loved us, how could He allow the disease to touch Kristina? As the tears began to flow down my face I continued to pray, "Father, you know how much I love her. I believe you sent her to me to teach me love. Why are you allowing this to happen to us?" I continued to cry out, "God, haven't I done enough for you? I have served you every way I felt you asked me."

For several minutes I let my self-centered anger flow from my mouth. As I continued to vent my anger, my tears ran down my cheeks and I became more calm. I prayed, "Father, please, I beg, wash this away from Kristina, make her healthy and strong again. I know if it is your will she can be healed completely. Show your great power and glorify yourself through her."

And as I gazed upon the tabernacle, trying to wipe the tears from my face, a strong voice filled me: *"Do not be afraid. Trust me. I will take care of my daughter."*

My breath was taken away and a sense of peace washed over me.

I had never before felt such a strong sense of God speaking directly to me, but I had no doubt at that moment that is precisely what I just heard. It was so clear and strong, so full of peace that I am not sure to this day that it was just an inner voice and not a real and audible voice that filled that room. Immediately, a sense of peace washed away my tears, the fear vanishing from my heart like darkness exposed to a bright light. I saw all my venting anger to be simply fear now all put aside by that strong presence of peace that had washed over me. The tears ended. I couldn't believe what I had just heard: "I will take care of MY daughter." Not "I'll take care of *your* daughter," but "I will take care of *my* daughter." At that moment I knew beyond doubt that Kristina was truly a beloved daughter of God the Father. He created her and loved her infinitely more than I could ever imagine. I thought I loved her as much as any person could be loved, but in that moment I knew how wrong I was. I knew that no matter how much I loved her, God loved her beyond all my human comprehension. She was His daughter. From the beginning of time she was His, only loaned to my care for a time. I knew He would be present and that He would take care of Kristina. We only had to trust Him.

CHAPTER FIVE

With the decision to not wait for egg harvesting, the first IV steroid treatment was scheduled by the nephrology office the following week. The hospital isn't far from our home, just a 30-minute drive, so the whole procedure would be about a half day door to door. I planned to take the first day, Wednesday, off from work to take her to the appointment. This would give us a chance to find the office in the hospital and for me to be there to support her during this first treatment. Kristina's grandmother, my mom, would take her the second day, and my wife, Kristina's stepmother, would take her for the final treatment on Friday.

The first day started bright and clear. Everything seemed calm on the way to the hospital, though I knew how stressed I felt deep down. I couldn't allow myself to show any of that to my daughter. I had to stay calm and relaxed so she would be able to draw upon my strength, even though I wasn't feeling that strong. I looked at Kristina knowing that she must have been just as much afraid as I was but she didn't show it at all. I prayed she could draw upon my calm and that everything would go well today.

We arrived at the hospital about thirty minutes early for the appointment. I felt we needed extra time to make sure we could find the correct department and get any paper-work done they might need before the treat-ment. We actually found a parking spot in the garage right next to the door and the elevator to take us to the outpatient department was right inside that door. Finding the floor was simpler than we thought—when we stepped off the elevator, the outpatient department was just down the hallway. We joked that we would have to wait forever now since we were so early. Kristina teased me that she always expected that when she went somewhere with me: I am habitually very early for everything.

We walked up to the department and were greeted by the smiling face of the IV nurse.

There was no doubt Janet knew what she was doing. She warmly greeted Kristina with a calm confidence that helped wash away our nerves. Though we didn't have any idea what was going to happen next, Janet not only knew what she was doing but was ready for Kristina herself. She really gave us the sense that, even though this was a large IV department, Kristina was her only patient, the only person in the department who mattered to her at this moment. This nurse was exactly who we needed at this stressful time.

Janet sat Kristina down in a comfortable lounge chair and pointed out the features of her IV area. She then calmly started to explain the procedure she was to undergo.

Kristina up to this point had always been terrified of needles. Her last blood draw took twice as long because of her nervousness. But Janet was such a calm professional that I could see those nerves vanish from Kristina as the nurse's sense of ease just flowed into her. She explained that all the medicine was ready to go in the department already. She would begin by putting the IV in and after the IV medicine was hooked up to the tube the procedure would probably take about ninety minutes. She explained how the steroid IV would work once it was in Kristina's body and warned her that it was very common to have a coppery taste in her mouth for a few hours once the IV started.

Again, Kristina has always been nervous about needles, but Janet was so calm and exceptionally skilled at her job that I don't know that Kristina even really noticed the IV go into her arm.

So for the next ninety minutes we sat and relaxed while the IV medicine was slowly dripping. Kristina did comment very early on that it gave a horrible taste in her mouth. I had never known before today that an IV could be tasted. It seems sort of odd to me. But it gave us another discussion point to fill the time.

Kristina has always been an avid reader, so she spent a majority of the time reading a new book. Mostly I sat there staring at the pages, unable to focus on the words before me.

The time passed without incident, and we left the hospital after taking a bit longer to figure out how to get back to our minivan. Funny how it seemed so easy to go from the minivan to the infusion department, but was so difficult to figure out how to get back to the minivan afterward. All Kristina could think about was getting back to her purse to get some chewing gum for that horrible taste in her mouth.

The next morning, grandma showed up and took Kristina to the hospital IV department. Kristina was greeted by the same nurse and everything went very well again. The pair spent the afternoon together and went to lunch after the IV was completed.

Day three brought the final treatment in the late morning. Kristina and her step-mom planned to complete the IV therapy and get home to make dinner before I arrived home from work. Again they arrived at the IV department and were greeted warmly by the same team of nurses. By this time not only were they very friendly but now they were familiar faces. They talked to Kristina comfortably while they inserted her final IV and set up the steroids. The therapy went smoothly again, but as they neared the end of the treatment Kristina began to complain about a sharp jaw pain. After the nurses checked her for a few minutes they decided it would be best to send her down to the emergency room to have her checked more closely by the doctors.

Connie called me at work to tell me they were moving Kristina to the ER for evaluation due to the sharp jaw pain. I immediately left work—but working in downtown Pittsburgh and being subject to public transportation to get home to my car and then drive to the hospital I was more then ninety minutes away. I left work praying for Kristina's health, afraid of what might be happening with her but comfortable at least that Kristina was in the care of the ER doctors and accompanied by Connie. I knew she would update me on any developments while I was in transit.

Two hours later I arrived at the Washington Hospital ER and was taken straight back to Kristina's room by the nursing staff. Connie updated me on the situation at the time. The doctors had drawn labs and were waiting for everything to come back. So we waited. Kristina seemed fine, except for the jaw pain of course. Finally, the doctor came into the room and told us the labs had come back and showed Kristina's potassium was dangerously high.

Your body needs potassium, which is an electrolyte. But too much potassium can be deadly. Hyperkalemia—the condition of having too much potassium in the blood—can cause cardiac arrest. They start to worry about cardiac arrest when the level of potassium in your blood is 6.0 mEq/L (milliequivalents per liter). Kristina's potassium level was 6.9. The doctors decided the best course of action would be to first treat Kristina with a medicine called Kayexalate, which carries excess potassion out of the body, and then admit her overnight for observation. The doctors said that after the medicine worked they would redraw labs and check her potassium levels to make sure they had come down to normal and stabilized within the safe range.

The nurse came in with two small cups of the creamy fluid and warned Kristina first that the Kayexalate tasted bad so it would be best to try to get it down fast. Second, she told Kristina that within thirty minutes or so she would start having to go to the bathroom. This would void the potassium from her body and bring the levels of potassium in her blood steam to a more normal and safe level. Well, Kristina left no doubt that the Kayexalate

was as bad tasting as advertised. As she finished drinking the Kayexalate the nurse
came into the room and advised us that a
room had been found on the renal floor of the
hospital and they'd be moving her shortly.

As they prepared to move Kristina to her
hospital room the nurses explained that she
would be on a renal diet for the length of her
stay in order to help her kidneys. Connie and
I decided that she would go home to take care
of the other kids and update them on the situation with their sister, while I stayed with
Kristina for the night. Connie and I stepped
outside the ER room as they were preparing
Kristina to move and said goodbye for the
evening.

Kristina and I moved up to her new room
and tried to get comfortable. Kristina was
tired but the Kayexalate started working so
she started making trips back and forth to
the bathroom while I settled into the lounge
chair the nurse brought into the room for me.
It was Friday night so we sat back and
watched a movie, trying to make the best of
the situation. The night passed without issues but also without much comfort. The

lounge chair just wasn't a great substitute for my bed at home.

We were woken up early by the lab technician when she came into the room to draw another set of labs. We hoped the potassium levels would be better this morning. But unfortunately though improved Kristina's potassium level was still very elevated at 6.1 mEq/L. The doctor informed Kristina that she would have to do another round of the Kayexalate. This news nearly made Kristina cry. She explained again how horrible the Kayexalate was and that she wasn't even sure she could manage to keep it down. But she had no choice in the matter, so she fought through and managed to drink the two cups of the medicine.

Not long after, a friend from our couples' study group who is a doctor and resident at the hospital stopped by Kristina's room to check on her. Connie had gone home the night before and sent an email to the couples in our group to tell them what was going on with Kristina and ask for prayer. Bruce's wife saw the email that morning and called him at work to tell him that Kristina was in his hospital. He finished his rounds and found her room. He was truly a godsend. While the doctors and nurses on staff were doing an excellent job updating us on everything, with Kristina's condition we still seemed to be in the dark on exactly what was happening.

Bruce came to her room and talked to us for a few minutes to try to explain. He asked to look at her records, and with Kristina's permission left the room to go to the nurse's desk and check her doctor's notes. He came back a short while later, sat down with us and tried to explain in terminology and words that we could understand. He said the other doctors should be back in a few hours to draw more labs.

When I say Bruce's visit was a godsend, I mean it. The feeling of not really understanding what was happening, combined with a bit of anxiety, doesn't make for a relaxing day at the hospital. Simply seeing a familiar and friendly face brightened our moods quite a bit. And then to have someone we know well and trust sit down and explain Kristina's condition in a way that we could understand took a lot of stress off of our shoulders.

A few hours later a lab technician came back again to draw more labs. Kristina's veins weren't very cooperative when trying to draw blood. They seemed to be deep, small or facing odd directions. So the lab sent a phlebotomist to Kristina's room who claimed to be one of the best in the hospital. After a quick search of Kristina's arm and an even quicker stick of the needle I think both Kristina and I had to agree with him. He really was very good at his jobDinner came and Kristina ate a nice, if somewhat bland, renal-specific meal while I sat back to watch the Penguins play a game of ice hockey on TV. We continued to wait for the results of the latest labs, hoping and praying they would come back normal and that we could go home soon.

Shortly after faceoff the doctor came in the room and told us that her potassium levels were within a safe and normal range. At Kristina's insistence the doctor agreed that she could go home as soon as he finalized the paperwork. Nearly an hour later we were walking out of the hospital, heading again toward our minivan. We were home before the third period of the hockey game started. After a quick snack and a warm, relaxing shower, Kristina was curled up snug in her bed. I didn't last much longer.

CHAPTER SIX

Now that we moved past this unexpected hospital stay we tried to fall back into a routine. Of course the new routine included some strong medications—a high dose of steroids to help keep down the inflammation caused by the lupus on Kristina's kidneys, CellCept (the chemotherapy drug) to help combat the lupus itself and a dozen other medications and vitamins. We had heard a lot about how the steroids would cause a lot of side effects for Kristina—some being an increased appetite and risk of weight gain and another being problems sleeping. Kristina really struggled to sleep for sure. And when she did she often woke with horrible nightmares. I guess one could only expect the nightmares when combining a strong medicine like the steroids with the fears a young girl would feel with a life-changing new diagnosis. The appetite, on the other hand, didn't seem to increase. On the contrary she didn't seem to be hungry as often. She often would walk away from the dinner table having only eaten half her meal. But despite this Kristina held her weight or even gained a little. We figured this was all due to the fact that she was eating smaller meals more often.

As Christmas approached we made plans to attend midnight Mass on Christmas Eve. Father Sam's love and reverence made the Mass extra special. Christmas was a relaxing day with family, celebrating the birth of our Savior. But this December 23rd changed our plans and our lives.Kristina wasn't feeling well so she decided to go to bed a little bit early that night. Her mom and I told her we loved her and said goodnight as she went to brush her teeth and get ready for bed.

I sat back with my wife to watch a Steelers game that evening and maybe even channel hop to the Penguin game on a different channel. Shortly after Kristina went to bed, I received a text from her on my phone telling me that her chest hurt and she was having trouble catching her breath.

I went right to her room to check on her. She showed me that her chest was hurting from about the area where her neck and shoulder came together on the left side down to the bottom of her ribs. She said she was having trouble breathing as well. So after a few minutes it was decided we would take Kristina back to the emergency room. Chest pain and trouble breathing just screamed heart attack to me.

We helped Kristina into the van and made the drive to the emergency room, arriving shortly after 8:00 p.m. The hospital staff moved Kristina right into triage and took her vital signs. Everything was pretty much in the normal ranges. They quickly moved her back to a treatment room and hooked her up to the heart monitors. Within minutes a technician arrived to do an EKG and a lab tech came to draw some vials of blood for the doctor all while the nurse checked Kristina into the ER, getting her list of medications in the computer.

It's funny how quickly things change. Not long before, Kristina had trouble just giving a little blood for a physical. Now she was already growing so used to nurses sticking her with needles for blood that she barely noticed any longer. We waited in the ER for the results. The doctor finally came into Kristina's room and explained that the lab work looked pretty normal, but they were concerned about the chest pain so they had decided to admit her for observation. Since it was so close to Christmas, the hospital would be partly shut down to accommodate the staff taking time off to celebrate the holidays, so it would take some time to find a room for her. By the time they finally found a room and moved her it was nearly 2:00 a.m.

The following morning the doctor on staff came in to speak with Kristina. He explained that they weren't sure what was causing the chest pain but that the labs and EKG were clear. They wanted to do an echocardiogram to get a good view of her heart to make sure there was no fluid buildup. He would order some pain medicine for her to help control the pain in her chest, he said the best thing he could order for her was morphine. Morphine was chosen mostly because it was kidney friendly.

Well, the echocardiogram came back clear later that morning—it did show a little fluid around the heart but according to the cardiologist that wasn't enough to be concerned about.

Shortly after we heard these results, her nephrologist came into the room for a visit. He wasn't on duty but had heard she was admitted and wanted to come see how she was doing. He explained that they thought she might have been retaining some fluid in her abdomen and that the fluid could be causing pressure on her diaphragm, which in turn could be causing the pain in her chest. He told us the amount of protein being dumped through Kristina's urine was very high and because of that protein loss she could expect to retain some fluid. Her Lasix medication should help her kidneys with that. He explained until they could explain and control the pain Kristina could expect to stay in the hospital, at least a couple of days. That would mean Christmas in the hospital.

We called home and updated the family, who immediately made plans to come to the hospital to visit Kristina on Christmas morning—bringing some Christmas treats and gifts for her to enjoy, but mostly bringing the love only a family can give.

That evening as Kristina dozed I sat and watched *It's a Wonderful Life*, a Christmas tradition for me through the years. But having not really slept the night before, I soon found myself dozing as well.

I think it must be a hospital tradition that sleep doesn't last long before the doctor comes back in the room. He didn't wake Kristina, but he wanted to check in with me and answer any questions we might have. He did a good job explaining everything they had seen in Kristina's labs and basically said if we wanted to go home there was no reason that she absolutely had to stay. He did recommend she stay for a short time so they could help control her pain more effectively with the IV morphine they could give her. I tried to convince myself to take her home and celebrate Christmas in our house, but knew that it was safer for Kristina to stay where she was. At least here they could control the pain more effectively and make sure nothing else was going on.

Lying back down in an attempt to go back to sleep, I began to think about missing all we had planned for Christmas. Midnight Mass was just starting about this time, morning would bring a sterile room instead of a warm home with a beautifully decorated tree. The tradition of opening gifts first thing in the morning with the kids was replaced with a cafeteria breakfast. But then it struck me that Christmas was about more than breakfasts, gift wrap or trees. Christmas was about love. And this Christmas was all about love, nothing more added to it. Simply love of a father for his daughter and love of a daughter seeing her father sitting at her side.

Christmas morning came early as that hospital tradition of waking everyone came about again. The lab technician was in the room while it was still dark outside to draw more labs while the nurse checked Kristina's vital signs and gave her a quick evaluation.

A few hours later, our family arrived, mom, brother, sisters and grandma came in like the wise men bearing gifts, love and prayers. They also brought a few treats from home to enjoy throughout the day as well.

The next few hours were great. Kristina laughed and told the story of her stay so far. Her siblings doted over their big sister and mom smiled and watched the scene. But finally that time had to come to an end and everyone had to leave. Again, Kristina and I were left with a quiet room. Kristina had time to take a nap, which was especially nice because the day's events seemed to have worn her out quite a bit.

The rest of the weekend went by much the same: too-short visits from home and long hours of just sitting around with little to do but wait. The pain never quite seemed to subside, but it was controlled.

Finally, Monday afternoon, her nephrologist came in to check on her again. He said they still thought the issue she was having might be related to some fluid in her abdomen that an X-ray had shown. He said they would decide for sure in the morning but they were thinking about draining some of the fluid off. He said the procedure wouldn't be a big deal: a simple insertion of a drain needle to remove the fluid, then she'd probably be able to go home shortly after that. He fully expected her to be home by Tuesday afternoon.

That night Kristina and I talked and decided that since it was so late in the year and I really had no time to take off from work remaining that I would go home so I could go into work the next morning. Connie and grandma would be in as early as they could to stay with her then bring her home. And that I would see her when I got home from the office that evening. We would open her Christmas gifts then and celebrate Christmas as a family, just a little belated.

CHAPTER SEVEN

I was awake early the next day, and went to the office to catch up on the reports and work that built up over the long holiday weekend. I spoke to Kristina early just to say good morning; she was tired and just waiting for mom and grandma to come, really hoping to be out of the hospital sooner than later that day. I called my wife and we talked for a short while about how my day was going so far. She was waiting for my mother to arrive at the house then they'd be on the way to the hospital. A few hours later my cell phone rang. It was my wife. I figured she would update me on the doctor's plans for the procedure or maybe that they weren't going to do the procedure and just send her home. I never expected to hear the words that I did.

I answered the phone but my wife's response was panicked, though she was trying to seem calm for me. "Ed, Kristina had some severe pain in her back this morning shortly after we got here. The doctors are worried she may have a blood clot in her lung."

She told me that the nurses called the doctors into Kristina's room shortly after they arrived and the doctors kicked them out of the room so they could have space to examine her. She went on to explain that the doctors were looking to do some tests to see if they could confirm whether a blood clot was present. Connie didn't know how long it would be before we found anything out. She thought the doctors were discussing transferring Kristina to a larger acute -care hospital downtown, but she wasn't sure yet. I asked if I should leave work and come to the hospital, but knowing how long it would take to get there we quickly decided that I should wait in my office downtown for an update. If the doctors moved Kristina to Montefiore hospital downtown, Connie and my mother would just come by my office and pick me up, and we'd all go to the new hospital together.

I hung up the phone in a panic. I had no idea what to do now. I couldn't concentrate on work—my daughter was in distress and I wasn't there to help her. The only thing I could honestly think to do at that moment was pray. So I sat for a few moments in my chair and asked God to take care of Kristina and keep her safe.

As I finished my prayer I felt a strong urge and need to call out for prayers from others. Being at work I didn't have all the phone numbers of the friends I wanted to ask for prayers. I could only think to text one friend who I knew was at work at the time. I sent Bob, one of my closest friends a simple text: "Brother, I need prayers. Kristina is being rushed to Montefiore due to an emergency."Bob answered my need by multiplying my request. We belong to a group of Christian men called Emmaus. Emmaus is basically a retreat that we sponsor twice a year to help other men find the Holy Spirit and a relationship with Jesus Christ. I've seen the Emmaus retreat do some spectacular things through the last few years that I've been involved, but nothing greater for me than the bond of brotherhood it gave me with many new brothers in Christ. Bob received my text and after a quick prayer sent an email blast to our whole Emmaus community. And they answered by praying and calling just wanting to help in any way they could.

Talk about quick action! Within no more than 10 minutes my phone rang. Another very close friend was calling to find out what was going on with Kristina and what he could do to help. I hung up the phone and just minutes later it rang again—another close friend asking the same question. Mark told me he works near Montefiore and he would be on the way to the hospital and meet us there. I tried to tell him not to take the time, I would call him if we needed anything more, but he insisted. Within twenty-five minutes of sending the text to Bob, I had received five calls asking what they could do for Kristina, for me and for my family. Some offering prayer while on the phone with me, all pouring out their love and pure desire to help upon us. There were a couple of people I had never met before, and I honestly was not sure if I had even heard their names.

Forty five minutes after Connie's first call she called back. She told me now that the doc-

tors had decided against transferring
Kristina by ambulance. They were in the
process of calling a Mercy Flight Medevac in
to rush her to Montefiore by air. They told her
they didn't want to risk the long drive and
that the helicopter would be much faster and
staffed by paramedics and nurses who could
handle any airborne emergency.

The doctors told Connie that they still suspected a blood clot because of the symptoms,
but couldn't absolutely confirm anything.
They conveyed to her the direness of the situation: if there was truly a blood clot in
Kristina's lung, it could be life-threatening.
Mercy Flight.

I asked how Kristina was holding up, Connie told me that they had just recently been
allowed back in the room with her and simply
said that she was very scared. Connie and my
mother would be leaving as soon as they took
Kristina to the helicopter and would call me
when they came through the Fort Pitt Tunnel
leading into town, so I could go out and meet
them. Thirty-five minutes later I was standing on the side of the street as they approached. They pulled up and I jumped in at
the stoplight, and as quickly as that we were

on our way to the hospital. There were no new updates on Kristina's condition; she got in the helicopter without incident and based on the doctor's estimates was probably at Montefiore by now.

We arrived at the hospital a few minutes later and were directed to her room by the front desk. We went up an elevator then down a long hallway, followed by another elevator, and we were on the 8th floor. As we came down the last hallway approaching 8 West, we saw a couple of paramedics in flight suits pulling a stretcher toward us. Connie recognized that these were the paramedics on the helicopter with Kristina. We stopped for a short moment and asked how she was doing. The paramedics told us she handled the flight very well and had no problems in flight, and the nurses were now getting her situated in her bed. They wished her the best. We thanked them for taking such good care of our daughter and moved quickly to Kristina's room.

As we arrived at her door, we saw several nurses in the room, so we stopped, not wanting to get in their way. They saw us though and motioned for us to enter, saying they were just wrapping up their evaluation of Kristina.

As we came into the room Kristina saw us and smiled. I ran to her side and give her a hug and kiss fighting the urge to cry. I didn't want to cause my daughter more stress by showing fear or anxiety to her. Kristina told us about her flight in the helicopter and said she was feeling O.K., though her chest and back still hurt. She made us laugh when she told us she thought the one paramedic was new because he looked a bit green to her. She said the nurses would be back shortly to draw some more blood and give her something for the pain. Another nurse came into the room and said we'd need to step out for a few minutes while they did a chest X-ray and the doctor did her evaluation.

So Connie, my mother and I stepped into the hallway. Kristina's room was near the end of the hall with a nurse's station at the end of that hallway. Since the area was fairly open, we moved into this area and looked out the big windows overlooking the city of Pittsburgh. Under other circumstances this would have been an incredible view. We stood talking for a few minutes when I noticed my Emmaus brother, Mark, rushing down the hall toward us. I ran up and embraced him. Mark had seen the text from Bob requesting prayers for Kristina and left work immediately to be there for us, since he worked just a few blocks away from the hospital. I updated Mark on what the current situation was with Kristina: basically we knew nothing. He said he'd be sure to get word out to our Emmaus brothers so the prayers would be lifted up loudly and quickly for Kristina. We talked for a short while waiting for the doctor to finish up in Kristina's room.

The nurses came out and told us we could go back into the room. When we entered a doctor was in the room with Kristina. She explained their concern about the pain, and we updated the doctor on what little we knew about Kristina's condition. The doctor said they would be sending Kristina shortly for a CT and were waiting for the results of the blood work. Within minutes they took Kristina from her room and led us down to the advanced imaging department. We sat patiently while they took Kristina into the CT room.

The CT came back clear of any blood clots. They kept her on the monitors and in the step-down unit so she could have closer attention. Amazingly, at least to me, every nurse she had seemed not much older than Kristina. But they were all truly gifts from God. Their empathy and professionalism was outstanding and put all of us at ease.

She spent New Year's Eve in the hospital and watched the city's fireworks from the window of her hospital room. For the next few days the doctors ran tests and watched the results of her blood work. Nothing ever showed anything truly definitive, so no real plan could be developed for her care. We often heard that lupus is a tricky condition that can manifest itself in many ways. The doctors often end up chasing symptoms, never finding causes—much as we appeared to be doing now.

The doctors finally decided there wasn't anything they could do to treat her in the hospital, so they released her. We were very excited as we walked Kristina out of the hospital to our waiting car to take her home. We were so happy that the hospital was behind us now. It felt so great to help Kristina into the passenger seat of our van, seeing the hospital receding in the rear-view mirror. Kristina peacefully dozed off in the dark van and slept during our ride home.

CHAPTER EIGHT

Unfortunately, that wasn't the end of Kristina's hospital stays. Just days after she left the hospital she was back in the emergency room with extreme chest pain again. The doctors in the ER ran the full workup of tests again, gave her some pain medication then finding nothing they sent her home. She slept fitfully that evening while we sleeplessly prayed for healing. We didn't know what else to do. The following evening, January 16th, her pain came on even stronger— now located in her left shoulder, chest and right abdomen. the pain was so strong that she was in tears. My wife and I debated whether to call the ambulance or just take her to the emergency room ourselves. After a few minutes, we decided it was safe enough for me to take her myself. We loaded her into the van and I took her back to the hospital emergency room. On the way, the pain was so extreme that she was nearly blacking out at times. I kept talking to her and regretted not calling the ambulance.

Finally, we arrived at the ER and I carried her from the van to the nurse's station. The nurses barely hesitated, checking Kristina in and moved her quickly into a room. Kristina was now in extreme pain but the doctors didn't want to give her any medicines to control the pain until they did some tests to try to determine the cause. This left Kristina in severe pain for a couple of hours while the doctors waited for all the results to return from the lab and radiology. It also left me with a lot of time to pray and worry about her.

I experienced that evening the worst pain a parent can experience—watching your child suffer and know there is absolutely nothing that you can do for her. I wished so desperately that I could take all the pain away from her. But I couldn't. All I could do was simply sit beside her bed, hold her hand and pray. I called my wife to give her an update on the situation. Not that there was much to say, but at that moment I felt very alone and very afraid. I thought to send a text message out to some friends asking them to pray for Kristina.

As I held her hand praying and asking God for the pain to be taken away, Kristina finally began to doze off and rest some. But I could tell by the look on her face that the pain had never relinquished its hold over her. Her face told of pain only pushed aside by exhaustion.

Understand that there is no way I can convey in words the experience that occurred next that night.

While she dozed I prayed. I had no clue what was wrong: all I had was prayer. I prayed from as deep within my soul as I ever have. I was leaning against her bedside, holding her hand and praying for a few hours when I looked up at Kristina's face.

Her face slowly softened, the pain seeming to ease and tears started flowing down her cheeks.

I asked her if she was all right or needed anything.

She simply and quietly replied, "He's nice.'

I asked her, "Who is nice?"

In reply she answered, "He's very nice." Her whole posture seemed more relaxed.

Just trying to keep her relaxed, I asked again, "Who is very nice?"

After a few moments she answered me with a single word: "Jesus."

I smiled and told her, "Of course He is. You know He loves you."

Her reply blew me away. She said, "I know. He told me. He's right here.""*What?*"

She said, "Yes, daddy, He's right here beside me." (She pointed to the other side of the bed) He's holding my hand."

I looked up to the corner of the room she had pointed at, all I could think to say was, "*What? Where?*"

She calmly replied "Yeah, He's really nice. He said He loves me and that I'm going home soon."

My tears flowed in a torrent of terror as those words struck me. *"What?"* You can imagine my fear of the "home" she was talking about. I was terrified that Christ had come to take her with Him and that I would lose my daughter that night. My terror flowed from my soul like the tears down my face.

"*What?* What did He say, baby? You are go— go...going home?"

Kristina replied, "He said not to be afraid, Daddy. He said everything will be OK.. I am going home." My tears continued to flow, and she continued, "With CJ, Samantha, Kaitlyn, mom and Buddy." (Buddy was our dog.) "He said don't be afraid, everything was going to be all right. If we trust Him everything will be okay."

My tears were flowing freely as I replied, "He told you everything will be OK? He is here now? He told you that?"

She replied, "Yes, He said everything will be all right. Just trust Him and don't be afraid."

She stopped talking and peacefully went to sleep. As I sat beside her with my head bowed in prayer, I looked down and saw a puddle of tears at my feet. I prayed thanks to God for the words she shared with me, and from the depths of my love for Kristina I praised Him for taking care of her.

CHAPTER NINE

Shortly afterward, the nurse came in the room and asked how Kristina was doing. I told her she was sleeping finally, but I couldn't tell her the reason for Kristina's peaceful sleep. The nurse told me the doctors had decided to transfer Kristina back to the hospital downtown because her primary doctors were there and they were better equipped to help treat Kristina. After a few hours of coordination, the ambulance finally pulled away with me right behind in our van.

As I followed the ambulance my mind raced thinking of the events that had occurred just a few hours earlier. At 3:00 a.m., after hours of stress, all kinds of thoughts ran through my mind. The one thing I can really remember of that rode into Pittsburgh was the sense of peace in my soul.

Early the next morning as the sun came up she woke up. I asked her if she remembered what happened. She said that she didn't remember anything from the previous night. I conveyed some of what had occurred. I didn't tell her many details because I could see that Kristina was upset she didn't remember. I guess a part of me was still trying to come to grips with the events from the previous night. I was sad though that she didn't remember such a remarkable experience. I knew I would never forget anything about those moments. The thought crossed my mind that maybe this vision had occurred to console me through her, I pushed that back quickly, though, since it sounded somewhat self-centered.

I went home that evening to shower and try to get some rest. I had to work in the morning. I told my wife, Connie, everything that had happened the previous evening. She was truly taken aback by the details I conveyed. Though I had told her about it by phone earlier, seeing my face and the conviction in my eyes left no doubt in her mind that it had really happened. I told her this was something I felt I had to keep in the privacy of my heart right now. It was just too big and personal to share openly with anyone else. She told me she felt the opposite—that this was a divine revelation to be shared with the world. She had no doubt this would give hope to many who heard this testimony.

Despite not having had slept for over 36 hours, I found it hard to relax that evening.

The following afternoon I got to Kristina's room after work. She told me, "Dad, I napped today and had a dream about Jesus." My heart leaped, and I think Kristina must have seen my reaction because she quickly continued, "It wasn't a vision, just a dream. But when I woke I remembered everything that happened Sunday night."

Kristina went on to tell me what had happened Sunday evening, moment by moment in exact detail. The only difference was that now I was hearing from her side.

She said she was trying very hard to relax and sleep but all she could feel was the intense pain and fear of what was wrong. Suddenly, a warmth washed over her. She opened her eyes and saw a man walking into the room. He approached her and stopped on the left side of her bed. She couldn't see His face because there seemed to be a bright light behind His head, something that reminded her of a sun-lit halo. All she could see was the man's silhouette. She knew I was to her right side because she could feel me holding her hands and hear my whispered prayers.

The man reached down and took her hand, gazing at her and said, "Kristina, do you trust me?"

She asked, "Who are you?"

He replied, "Do you know who I am, Kristina?"

She said, "I don't recognize you. But your voice. —I know your voice, don't I? Tell me your name—who are you? Why do I know your voice?"

Not answering, He replied, "Kristina, do you trust me?"

She asked, "You're Jesus, aren't you?"

Again not answering, He squeezed her hand ever so softly as He repeated, "Kristina do you trust me?"

She answered, "Yes, Lord, I trust you."

He said, "Kristina, if you trust me, then be not afraid, for I am with you always."

She said, "But I am so scared!"

He replied, "Kristina, do not be afraid. Everything will be OK. I am always with you.

You're going to go home soon and everything will be all right."

He again affirmed, "Trust me, Kristina, everything will be all right. You will be going home with your family, to be with CJ, Samantha, Kaitlyn, your mom and Buddy."

And, suddenly He was gone. The room looked normal. She turned her head and saw me looking at her, then closed her eyes and slowly fell asleep. She said she knew the pain was still there, but now somehow it felt distant and strangely disconnected.

Many words from Scripture came to my mind as I sat there that evening watching Kristina sleep peacefully in her hospital bed. "My sheep know my voice; I know them, and they follow me"—that meant my daughter "knew His voice," so that meant she was His, right? As I pondered that thought I really felt uplifted. If Kristina knew His voice, then, as this verse says, she was His sheep. I really felt a sense of excitement and peace at this thought. To this day this brings a smile and peaceful feeling when I think of these words.

"Be not afraid." I've heard that this is written 366 times throughout the Bible. I don't know where to find many of those 366 times

—I'm not even sure that is a true count. I do know, though, that the one time He spoke those words to me will ever change me. The hymn came rushing to mind and I began to sing, "Be not afraid. I go before always. Come follow me, and I will give you rest."

Lastly, in that dark and lonely hour I thought of the words from Matthew 28, "And be sure, I am with you always." Somehow these words didn't seem very abstract any more. The events of the evening brought these words to truth like never before.

CHAPTER TEN

The following evening, after visiting Kristina, I went to the small chapel in the hospital before going home to try to get some rest before returning to work the next day and starting the routine all over again. As I knelt before the altar, I couldn't stop thinking about the words I heard just weeks earlier when on retreat. It felt like it had been years since I heard the words God impressed upon me. "I will take care of my daughter." The knowledge that my baby girl heard the voice of Christ and saw His face was now a conduit of peace to me.

I knelt and prayed—not prayers of need or fear, but at this quiet moment I praised God for His glory and love. I gave Him all my heart in thanksgiving for the peace He has given me in the darkest hours. As I knelt there, more Holy Scripture came to mind to lift me up. "Even though I walk through the valley of the shadow of death, I shall fear no evil," and "Be still and know that I am God." I had never thought in my worst nightmares that I would start to have a grasp of Psalm 23. But now I thought that I was now walking in that dark valley and saw the face of darkness and fear. Yet in this moment I didn't feel a sense of desolation. On the contrary, I was feeling strong consolation in the Lord. I knew if I could stay focused when the valley seemed darkest and most frightening, when I was feeling most alone, Jesus Christ would come down to the depths of the valley of death to find me and pull me out.

I didn't know what to pray as I continued to kneel in that small chapel. I felt empty of the words to say to thank God for what He has done. My deepest prayers conveyed my fear to Him for Kristina's health and ongoing struggles with the lupus within her.

Slowly, I felt my prayer move back to intercessory prayers on behalf of my beloved daughter. And as my mind raced to the fears of the moment, I found Him speaking to me again, simply telling me to "be still, know

that I am God." In those moments of prayer
God came to me with the words of Psalm
46:10, my favorite verse from the Bible. And I
could feel my spirit calm and His peace come
upon me. Romans 8:28 came into thought
then as I knelt there alone: "In all things God
works for the good of those who love Him."

Funny that this verse should come to me
now. I hadn't even known it a few months earlier—not until the men in my Saturday morning faith group taught it to me. We had discussed faith and joy in times of trouble and
strife. Little did anyone know on that Saturday morning that God would be giving me
these words to uplift me and give me strength
just a few months later. "In all things God
works for the good of those who love Him"—
words of strength to deal with all that would
come along with a mind and heart to giving
Him glory in all that I did.

Connie waited up for me to come home that
evening, though it was already late. I gave
her an update on Kristina and told her of our
daughter's further revelations of her visit two
nights earlier. As I told her what Kristina had
shared with me, she was amazed—not that
this had happened but by how it made her

feel. She told me to be strong and know that God is there. "He has given us such a gift that so few have been blessed to receive: His own presence and words."

Connie told me about her day at work and how she couldn't help telling everyone what had happened with Kristina Sunday evening. She told the story to those in her office, and watched as amazed eyes opened wider and some tears started to fall. She told me that sharing what had occurred with her co-workers had uplifted them and given them a strong sense of hope. Connie said that after she had told them what had happened that night many of them were very excited at the reality of Christ.

That really made me think a lot about everything and re-evaluate in my heart the personal nature of these revelations and this visit. I knew at that moment that, if given the opportunity to speak of His visit and blessing that evening, I would not be able to resist telling the whole world.

Lying in bed that night, I pondered the blessing of our Lord's coming to be with His daughter in her time of need. I can't grasp how blessed we are because of those few moments. And I can only attribute this visit to the pure heart of my daughter and to the prayers being offered to His Throne for her by those who answered my text request for prayer a few hours earlier that evening. I thank all my brothers and sisters who offered prayers for Kristina that evening. Because, while I was struggling to think straight, their prayers rose to God and brought Him to come to my daughter and give her rest. He came to me through her to give me peace and joy in a dark hour.

The following day I was at work very early to try to get things done so I could get back to Kristina as early as possible. I felt so horrible having to be at work while she was at the hospital alone. At lunch I decided I would attend daily Mass at St. Mary of Mercy Church, just a few blocks from my office.

As I was leaving, I ran into a friend near the elevator. She asked how Kristina was doing and told me that her family continued to pray for her every day. Suddenly I found myself pouring out the story of that evening's events. I told her of the pain Kristina was in and how suddenly the pain seemed to vanish as a sense of calm came over her. I told her about the dread I felt when Kristina told me she was going home and the surprise and exhilaration I felt when she told me that Christ Himself was standing beside her and telling her all would be OK.

Over the next twenty minutes I told her everything that had happened forty-eight or so hours earlier. She was enthralled by the story I was telling her. I could see in her eyes the fear I felt that night when Kristina told me she was going home, and the smile cross her face as I told her of Christ's uplifting words to Kristina to simply trust Him. She asked me if I had held Kristina's hand since that night, the hand that Christ had held. I was taken back for a moment, I hadn't even thought about that. I had sat all evening while Kristina slept after being transferred, holding the hand Christ had just hours earlier cupped in His hand. I felt tears start to come to my eyes as these thoughts passed through my mind.

When I was finished telling the story I felt a tap on my shoulder. Turning, I saw a man standing behind me with tears on his cheeks. He just stood there staring at me, unashamed of his very wet face. I didn't know what to say

—I was surprised and really off balance. He apologized for listening in to my story, but told me that it had moved him. We looked at each other for a few moments. Finally he said, "What you were saying, is that all true? Did it really happen?"

I told him that everything I had said was true and really did just happen two nights earlier.

He wiped his eyes on his sleeve and smiled at me. He explained that he had little need for God in his life and in fact though having been raised in a good Catholic home he hadn't been to Mass in nearly 20 years. "I haven't thought about God in a long, long time. Years, really. Now I don't know that I will ever be able to stop thinking about Him," he said. Still not knowing what to say I stood quiet for a moment. He looked up at me again and said, "I was just going to lunch when I happened to overhear what you were saying, at first I felt rude for eavesdropping, but the more you said the more I wanted to hear. And the more I heard the more I felt touched and felt a need to pray."

I told him that I had intended to go to noon Mass across the street at St. Mary of Mercy

and he was welcome to join me, We walked together to St. Mary of Mercy. Having missed
Mass already, we came into the church and
knelt together before the altar and simply
were quiet. Within moments I heard him crying again. I reached over and put my arm
around his shoulder to comfort him he simply
bowed his head and sobbed quietly. I could
see his lips moving in prayer so I remained
quiet. I prayed for the Holy Spirit to come
upon the man fully and to never let him go
again.

After several minutes he smiled and stood.
We walked out of the church together and
back to work. He told me he felt a new conviction to seek and find a relationship with Jesus, especially since now he knew in His
heart that Jesus is real and not just a story
from the Bible. He said he had always had
strong doubts about Christ's reality but that
was gone now. And I knew at that moment
that this story must be told.

I saw this man a few times over the next
months. The second or third time I saw him
he was in the cafeteria reading his new but
somehow already worn Bible. He told me that
his wife and daughter kept telling him how

amazed they were at his change in the past weeks. He hadn't missed Mass on Sunday, had started going to daily Mass and was reading the Bible like nothing he had ever read before. He had even asked his wife to re-new their wedding vows but this time in front of God as their witness. I can't help thinking how a few moments in one dark evening of my life lit a bright pathway for another soul.

CHAPTER ELEVEN

Kristina spent three more days in the hospital. The doctors still couldn't figure out what was causing the pain in her upper chest, throat and right side, but said it wasn't related to her heart in any way. Her blood pressure was a bit higher than they would like, but they said that could be an effect of the medicines. So they added another blood-pressure medicine to her daily regime and sent her home, blaming everything on the lupus—a theme that would be repeated many times.

On the way home we stopped at the pharmacy to pick up her new prescription. Kristina was in such high spirits and so excited to get home and have something good to eat. Somehow the hospital always found a way to put gravy on all her food, so she claimed. She hated that gravy. When we were called to the counter to get the medicine the pharmacist came up and greeted us. He smiled at Kristina and said his daughter told him we'd be coming by the pharmacy. Little did we know that Kristina's newest rheumatologist at the hospital was the daughter of her new pharmacist.

We really liked his daughter as a doctor— she had a great bedside manner, as they say. This new doctor was very young, not long assigned from medical school. She really took time to talk and explain medical terminology or big thoughts to us in a way that we could understand. She would take the extra time to explain not only what was being planned, but why the doctors were planning to do the tests. This gave us a lot of insight on Kristina's treatment and suspected conditions and really made us feel better the in months to come when we had to talk to new physician teams about what was going on and what had been done.

The new pharmacist was much like his daughter: he cared for his patients. He took the extra moments to smile and look them in the eye. I don't think he ever saw a patient as a customer. More likely he saw every patient he filled a prescription for as his family or friend, someone to care for as he would care for his own daughter. Just the next afternoon Kristina woke from a nap with a scream. She had been having nightmares, probably brought on by the steroids she was taking. Her nephrologist had warned the prednisone had many side effects.

As I helped her calm down, Kristina explained that the nightmare was of a beautiful woman standing beside her while she slept. The woman would say comforting words to Kristina. I could really see in Kristina's eyes the terror this event in the dream brought her. She went on to explain that the woman looked wrong somehow, maybe a little too pretty. Kristina said she felt a desire to be closer to the woman while at the same time a strong need to run away from her. And as the desire to get away would grow, Kristina could feel herself waking from the dream. As she would begin to wake, the woman would reach out to grab her. And, as Kristina would look up and focus on the woman, she would suddenly change to look like a corpse with horrible decayed hands and fingernails. Kristina told me that this woman had been in her dreams a lot lately, and that each time the woman would reach out to grab her there was a flash of light, the woman would scream and Kristina would wake up. It seemed such a vivid dream to Kristina, and I felt helpless to assist her. All I could think to do was pray God's protection around Kristina from the evil that appeared to be threatening her.

That evening Kristina had yet another attack of this extreme pain. She was having trouble breathing and was in tears because of how severe it had become. We had no choice but to go back to the emergency room again. By this time, the staff of the emergency room were beginning to know us pretty well. The nurse who came to the door of the emergency room to bring us from the waiting area to a treatment room rolled her eyes and remarked teasingly that we had to stop meeting like this. As we walked down the hallway to the room a doctor looked up and greeting Kristina like an old friend. Well, as much as we'd been in the emergency room lately it was beginning to feel a bit too comfortable.

As soon as Kristina was situated in the room the doctors had her set up on an EKG to

monitor her pulse, blood pressure and heart
rate to make sure there were no issues with
her heart. They also drew another set of the
same basic blood work.

At this point, between being a small girl,
the medications and having had so many
pokes to draw blood recently, Kristina's veins
were becoming much more difficult to find
and draw blood from. The emergency room
called in the special phlebotomist to do his
magic and get the tubes of blood they would
need. When he arrived you could tell his
whole persona was about making his patients
feel comfortable and relaxed. His eyes never
seemed to leave Kristina's, though they
deeply scanned her arms and hands for a
good vein. While he inserted the IV he
smiled and joked about the weather. I don't
know that Kristina was ever aware of the IV
being inserted until he was getting up to
leave the room. He explained to us what future phlebotomists need to do to help with
blood draws and IVs. He really understood
how to make his patient feel comfortable and
empowered.

The doctors advised up front that they
would recommend transferring Kristina back

to the downtown hospital. They simply weren't confident of diagnosing ailments or treating her lupus. Within the hour the blood work came back and showed some unusually high heart enzymes. This was very concerning, as the doctors explained these enzymes are often indicative of a heart attack. The EKG showed no heart rate or rhythm issues, but did read a slightly elevated blood pressure and high heart rate. The doctors did a great job explaining the tests, and with great warmth and concern they conveyed their concerns but also tempered those with positive indications.

So another evening passed while the doctors monitored and the hospitals coordinated the transfer and room. We sat waiting, nervousness was beginning to become second nature to me it seemed. Finally, several hours later, the room at the downtown hospital had been arranged, and we were told the ambulance would be there shortly to transfer her downtown. I gathered her personal items together in preparation for the ambulance's arrival. Kristina rested the best should could, catching a few minutes of sleep.

At nearly one o'clock in the morning, the ambulance arrived. With a warm, practiced, caring manner, the paramedics transferred the monitors and oxygen to the vehicle's transportable equipment, and then covered Kristina with freshly warmed blankets to fend of the few moments of Pittsburgh January between the emergency room door and the ambulance. The paramedics spoke to the doctors and nurse, then took Kristina's paperwork and were off, with me following closely behind.

When we arrived at the hospital, I made it up to the floor Kristina would be staying on before she did. The paramedics had to bring Kristina through the emergency room to check in so were delayed a short time while they checked Kristina into the new hospital. The nurse at the floor's nursing station took me to the waiting area at the end of the hall and said they would come get me as soon as Kristina arrived on the floor and the nurses checked her vital signs and got her settled in.

It was nearly three o'clock in the morning when she was finally in the room and I could join her. She was sleeping peacefully while I sat beside her in the chair provided trying to get a bit of rest. The EKG machine was again hooked up and displaying a constant rhythm, heart and blood pressure. Except from my extensive training watching medical shows on television, I really had no clue what I was looking at on the monitors. The nurses said she was stable and comfortable. There was a lot of ease in their manner and that brought me comfort. The nurse didn't have much information to provide but said the doctor would be in shortly to check on her and would be able to give us an update on what they were looking at and planning to do.

I had just dozed off when he finally came in. He quietly asked her some questions and checked her vitals and chart. He told us that he didn't know what the plans were; we would have to wait for Kristina's specialists to come in the next day, probably in the afternoon, on their normal rounds. He confirmed that Kristina was stable though her heart rate and blood pressure were elevated probably because of the stress and some of the medication she was on.

Breakfast came in the morning but Kristina wasn't in the mood to eat. In addition to having little appetite she really just wanted to sleep. It seems that the one thing a sick person needs, rest, is the one thing a sick person really can't do while in the hospital. There are just too many nurses, doctors and test to allow one a chance for a good night's sleep. So, I sat while she slept. I should have been able to get some sleep but I guess the stress was keeping me from relaxing. It's a good thing though because her new day nurse came in to do the normal vitals check and morning blood work.

This nurse was great. She was just a few years older than Kristina and was very empathetic and caring for her concerns. She really could relate to Kristina, since they were so close in age, and that helped Kristina more than we could know at the time. Nurse Kelly came in and smiled at Kristina then just talked to her. She really put Kristina at ease and took away a lot of the edge of fear she may have been feeling. They really seemed to hit if off right away. Nurse Kelly took time to get to know Kristina as a person more than just a patient, which means a lot when you're the father watching your sick daughter lie in a hospital bed hooked to monitors and IV tubes.

Kelly carefully went through the rather large list of medications Kristina was currently taking each day. At this time she was taking 18 different medications with upwards of 46 pills at some time during the day. A fact that really depressed Kristina especially since some of the pills tasted bad or were rather large and cumbersome to swallow. Kelly put all the medications in to the system so the pharmacy could get Kristina's daily medications to her as quickly as possible. Before she left the room, Kelly asked if she could do anything for Kristina. Though it was just 9:00 a.m., Kristina asked if she had any popsicles. Kelly grinned and asked "red or orange?" Within minutes Kristina's smiling lips were painted red.

By mid-afternoon, Kristina's rheumatology team finally came in to check on her during their rounds. The pharmacist's daughter was there along with the kind-hearted lead doctor. They smiled and asked Kristina what brought her back from this visit. She explained her symptoms and they talked about their thoughts and some plans the resident team had mentioned regarding her chest pain and heart rate. The most comforting news they had was that the last blood work showed only slightly elevated heart enzymes so their concern of a heart attack was low.

Right around dinnertime Kristina's mom and grandmother arrived for a visit. They brought with them a lot of smiles and a real change of atmosphere with them. Kristina's face lit up to see these particular visitors and the stuffed animal they carried with them.

While Kristina ate her dinner, a great smelling chicken meal which of course coated with a thick gravy, grandma, my wife and I went to the cafeteria to get some dinner as well. I hadn't realized until I walked into to the cafeteria that I hadn't eaten anything in over 24 hours. Everything looked and smelled great, not something you often say about hospital food. We talked about Kristina and what the doctors were saying. My mom asked a lot of details because she worked in another hospital in the cardiac department with one of the area's leading cardiologists. Grandma wanted to ask his input and thoughts so needed all the details.

When we arrived back in Kristina's room she had finished eating, though it really only looked like she had picked at the food on the plate. Kristina told us that the resident team had been in to examine her. She wasn't sure what their plans were for her with staying in the hospital but she asked them to come back when we were there to talk to us.

When they returned to her room about an hour later they told us that Kristina was stable and her blood work looked fairly normal. The lead doctor told us that they were concerned about her high heart rate and wanted to have a couple of tests done primarily a stress EKG to check her heart for any problems. They didn't know how long Kristina would be staying this time but said they wanted to make sure when she left she wouldn't be returning anytime soon.

Kristina was feeling somewhat nauseous so the doctor prescribed a medication called Compazine to help combat the nausea. The medication was inserted into her IV to have the quickest effects. It didn't take very long before Kristina started to feel better, her nausea lessening slightly. Within thirty minutes though, Kristina commented that her neck felt tight. I reached over and rubbed her shoulders and neck to help her relax. But this didn't help, in a matter of minutes her neck and shoulders locked up. Kristina began to panic; I tried to calm her while I called the nurse. The nurse came in the room and quickly called the doctor who was still on the floor. She came into the room and examined Kristina whose neck and shoulders were still locked. Kristina was crying and very visibly upset at this point. Another nurse came into the room and in a just a second told the doctor that Kristina was having a reaction to the nausea medication. The reaction was very rare, but could be treated quickly with Benadryl. The doctor nodded to the first nurse, who stepped out of the room for a few moments. When she returned she had a syringe with Benadryl to insert into Kristina's IV. Within moments Kristina's neck and shoulders relaxed and the reaction was over. To Kristina's credit she recovered from her panic quickly, making a joking comment that of course she'd be the one in a thousand to react to that medication.

Late that night after Kristina was deep in slumber I left to go home and get some sleep, cleaned up and a change of clothes. I had to go to work the next morning which worked out well since all Kristina would be doing was some tests and watching TV.

On the dark highway home I did the only thing I could think of at the time: pray. I asked God to take care of Kristina and take away this illness. In my conversation with God I recalled the woman from Scripture who had "the bleeding disease" and how His healing could wash away all illness with just a touch of His tassel. I knew deep within my heart that if God willed it Kristina would be healed. Not just healthy enough to go home, but completely washed free of the lupus.

But, when it came to the end of my prayer as I turned into my driveway, I couldn't say "Thy will be done." My prayer finished in the garage with me asking God that He understand how much I loved Kristina and that is the only reason I couldn't bring myself to say those words in my prayer. I knew God understood how I felt—after all, He sent His Son to earth, and then had to sit and watch His Son die at the hands of the very people to whom He sent His Son. Deep inside I was afraid that, if I gave over to His will, it might not go the way I wanted it to go. I knew He would understand, since He had already expressed

His deep love of Kristina. Little did I realize at the time the trap this prayer would become for me.

The next days were long and arduous, filled with work, driving and prayer. Not enough sleep for sure, and cafeteria food that had somewhat lost the luster it had that first evening. The stress EKG came back normal as well as the other tests. So, again Kristina was heading home, still with the same basic symptoms but with the knowledge that there was nothing the doctors could really do to treat her again. Those words we heard many times over the past months, and would hear often in times to come, were spoken again: "It must be the lupus. That is a tricky illness."

CHAPTER TWELVE

It seemed that Kristina was home only a very short time again before the chest and side pain came back stronger than before, again accompanied by shortness of breath and dizziness. We rushed back to the emergency room to find through the blood work that her potassium level was high again. The emergency room nurse brought in Kristina's favorite medicine, Kayexalate, the awful-tasting liquid that would lower her potassium levels quickly. She fought the creamy liquid down and we sat back waiting for it to work. Over the next several hours the doctors monitored Kristina's potassium levels while communicating with the rheumatology team downtown.

The doctors finally decided that while Kristina's potassium level was decreasing they were still going to transfer her back to the hospital downtown mostly because of the shortness of breath, elevated heart rate and muscle weakness she was experiencing. So again we made the midnight transit between hospitals.

The next morning, while waiting for the doctors to come in on their normal rounds, Kristina commented that she felt very light-headed then suddenly blacked out. I called the nurse to the room, who quickly assessed Kristina's vital signs and called another nurse to the room. The second nurse, more senior, quickly pressed the button on the wall behind Kristina that called an emergency condition. The last thing any father wants to hear or see is a hospital-wide medical alert over the announcement system for his daughter. The senior nurse told me that I would have to leave the room as there would be a lot of doctors coming in very fast and they would need room to work. She didn't tell me what was going on, just that Kristina was completely unresponsive and they needed to get the urgent-care teams in quickly to care for her.

I stepped out in the hallway and was quickly ushered away from the door as the first doctors arrived in the room. I dropped to my knees to pray for God's help now as the tears flowed down my face. When I thought of it, I called my wife at work and tell her what was happening. I was truly terrified. Connie told me she would leave work immediately and be at the hospital as quickly as she could. More doctors came into the room, some lingered in the doorway. I called my mother to let her know what was happening. She said she was leaving work shortly and would be on her way to the hospital as well.

Time seemed to be moving very slowly for me. I was in the hallway and had no idea what the doctors were doing with my daughter. But, finally, a doctor came up to me and told me Kristina was awake and seemed stable. They explained that after several attempts she simply regained consciousness. Now, she was afraid and wanted to see me.

Without hesitation or further permission I ran to her side and held her hand, putting my head close to hers, whispering that everything was OK now and that I loved her deeply. I vividly remember telling her, "Re-

member, Christ Himself told you that everything would be O.K.," at which Kristina
calmed a little bit and a slight smile appeared
on her lips.

Minutes later my wife arrived, just in time
for one of the critical-care doctors to ask us to
step into the hallway so he could speak to us.
He told us that they weren't sure what happened, but that Kristina's episode didn't seem
typical of someone passing out. They wanted
to get an EEG done to make sure she hadn't
had a seizure or some other problem with her
brain. He assured us again that she was stable now. His main concern was that Kristina
had suffered an atypical seizure, he called it a
pseudo-seizure. They would do their best to
determine what happened in those minutes,
but he wasn't confident that anything definitive would show unless they happened to
catch an episode while it occurred.

Very quickly a technician arrived with the
EEG machine, and again we were moved into
the hallway while she completed the test. We
sat in the small waiting area at the end of the
hallway and talked about what had just occurred, I tried to relate what I had seen and
felt during the whole "condition" that was

called on Kristina. I could only remember being very afraid and feeling alone while all the activity occurred around Kristina. Within a short time the EEG was completed and the technician was gone. Grandma came in the room to see how Kristina was doing now, and we sat and quietly relaxed while Kristina dozed in her bed.

The evening passed quietly—for a hospital, that is. The nurses came every 3 hours to draw blood and check Kristina's vital signs, each time waking us from the light sleep we had just drifted into. The nurses were always very apologetic and kind; they understood Kristina wanted and needed sleep, but their primary job was to make her better, and unfortunately that entailed regular interruptions to her sleep.

The next morning while Kristina ate breakfast we sat and talked. She couldn't wait to get out of the hospital; she really was beginning to miss being at home. As she reached out for a piece of the pancake that made up her breakfast I heard the fork drop from her hand and in mid-sentence Kristina blacked out again. I tried to remain calm and wake her. I could see her eyes moving under her closed lids but she wouldn't wake, so again I hit the nurse call button telling them she had blacked out again.

The nurse came back to the room quickly and checked Kristina while I held her hand. I talked to her trying to get her to wake up, but though her eyes seemed to be straining they simply didn't open. Then I saw a tear roll from the corner of her eye down her cheek as I heard the heart monitor alarm sound and again those words that I so dreaded: "Mr. Corbett, we are going to have to call a condition on Kristina. We're going to need to ask you to leave the room. Sorry."

I again stepped into the brightly lit hallway that seemed strangely dark to me as I watched the doctors begin to arrive in Kristina's room. I leaned back against the wall near the door and, trying to listen to what the doctors were saying, I prayed. "Oh God, you promised Kristina would be all right. Please don't forget that promise. Take this away from her, please." I was so afraid for my daughter, I really didn't understand what was happening and the fears raced through my head. I knelt down beside her door and said a quiet prayer. "Please, Lord, take care of your daughter." Everyone was focused on Kristina—I was alone in the hallway with my tears and prayers.

I continued to listen but heard no response from God—nor did I understand what I was hearing from inside the room. At least what I was hearing in the room didn't sound as hectic as it had a few moments earlier. Finally a nurse stepped out of the room. She looked at me and her face changed to one of empathy. I had been alone in the hallway for what seemed like an eternity, no knowledge of what was going on or if my daughter was alright or not. The nurse suddenly recognized my loneliness and fear. She asked if I was all right. Once she was sure that I was calm, she told me it was O.K. to come back in the room. Kristina was again awake and pretty scared.

Kristina told us that she could hear everything that was happening but she couldn't think straight, open her eyes or talk at all. She said she felt terrified and locked into the darkness that she couldn't escape. The doctors said they weren't sure what had happened but the EEG the day earlier had been clear, showing no signs of any seizure, stress, or problems.

The neurologist thought she might be suffering from pseudo-seizures, seizure-like events that aren't truly seizures at all. The doctors weren't sure how to treat these events, but knew the regular unit room was not the best place for her to be while they tried to figure it out. The doctors decided it was time to move Kristina from this normal room to a step-down unit. The difference primarily was a better nurse-to-patient ratio, so Kristina could get more personalized care and closer monitoring overall. The doctors told us that the staff of the step-down unit were more capable of handling emergency conditions that might arise, as the nursing staff was more readily available and had a higher level of training.

So, within a few hours, they moved Kristina to her new room. Another advantage of this new unit was that she was now in a private room instead of sharing a room with another patient. There was some hope that she might have the opportunity to get a bit more uninterrupted rest along with the higher level of care.

That evening her night nurse told her that the doctors had ordered some extra blood tests because they had seen a slight drop in her H&H, hemoglobin and hematocrit. Basically, Kristina's blood count had dropped slightly, but enough to make the doctors want to watch it a bit closer. Decreased H&H can signify anemia, and it can be dangerous if the level goes low enough.

The doctor came in and explained that Kristina's H&H was at 8.9, while a normal reading was between 12 and 16, with a more at-risk reading below 7.0. We asked what could cause the lower blood counts, joking that it seemed like all the lab draws the hospital does seemed to be likely culprit. He told us that there were numerous causes that were nothing to be concerned about, but that these lower levels were something to watch just in case. The doctor explained that lupus can cause a dangerous condition in which the red blood cells prematurely break down. The doctor said he would monitor her blood counts very closely over the next hours. Their attention to the blood work would help them determine what course of action might be necessary as well as if any other tests were required.

The following day, work went along without any problems, though in my tired mind time did seem to drag a bit. I guess my mind was so much on Kristina it was hard to concentrate on being at work. The best part of the day was that it was Friday, so the weekend should give me some rest at least. It didn't help that I had texted Kristina around breakfast and she hadn't answered by mid-morning. I really felt the stress and fear being apart from her. I imagined the worst scenarios.

Finally, late morning I called the nurses station to check on her. The nurse told me Kristina was resting and that they'd pass along my message to her. A little later, Kristina responded to my text and told me she really felt tired and dizzy, so she had been resting and missed my text message. I asked if the doctors had seen her yet that morning and what they had told her. She said they hadn't said a lot to her—just that they would come back later in the afternoon, after I arrived at the hospital.

It really helped that I would leave my office and be on the main roads to the hospital before traffic would pick up at the end of the workday. With the distance and timing, the hospital was no more than ten minutes from my office. It often seemed to take longer to get from the parking garage to Kristina's room navigating the halls and elevators than it did to drive the highway from my work to the hospital.

I arrived shortly after 4:00 p.m. each day, and today was no exception. I even got lucky and found a parking spot close to the main hospital entrance, so I didn't have to walk far from my car to get inside the hospital.

I walked into Kristina's room and found her resting with the television turned on. She woke when I entered and smiled at me. It felt good to see those big brown eyes and that great smile. After such a long day at work, I felt like I could finally take a deep breath; I was back where I had some control and knowledge of how Kristina was all the time.

I told Kristina that Saturday morning I wanted to go to my men's group early, but I would be in to see her about 10:00 a.m. That night after Kristina was settled with a kiss on the cheek, I left her in the care of the hospital staff and drove home.

I had to try to get some sleep. I had now
been five days with only an average of two to
three hours of sleep a night, if that. I felt confident now that Kristina was settled in and
very sure that she was in good hands until I
returned the following morning.

Prayer had really become my companion
while I made my drives to and from the hospital and work. I spent a lot of time questioning
God on why this would all be happening to a
girl who wanted so badly to give her life to
His service. I would ask God to give me the
strength to be all that Kristina and the rest of
my family needed in me. I didn't know what
that would mean, but I knew I had to be there
for all of them somehow. Mostly, though, I
prayed for Kristina's healing. I told God that I
wouldn't be opposed to a miraculous healing.
I learned on my rides home that I could pray
a Rosary using the steering wheel of van as a
guide. The wheel at 2 and 10 had screws on
the back side, and from those screws down to
the crosspiece were 5 finger grips on each
side. So I could pray my five Hail Mary
prayers down and five back up to the screw to
complete a decade. I found great solace focusing on the repetitive nature of this prayer and

even more focusing on the mysteries of Jesus' life and passion.

Kristina called me the following morning as I was leaving the church. She told me the doctor had just been in and told her that her H&H levels were still very low and had in fact dropped some during the night. The doctor told her he was going to order a blood transfusion to help raise her levels to normal. The nurse was already ordering the blood from the blood bank in the hospital. She told me how scared she was at the moment. I assured her that I was on my way and would be at the hospital as quickly as I could get there.

I walked into her room as the nurse was taking Kristina's vital signs in final preparation for the blood transfusion. I asked her for an update. The nurse explained that Kristina's 6:00 a.m. labs had shown her H&H levels had fallen to just 6.5. She explained that the blood was on the floor just waiting for them to start the IV, but that they needed to get some vitals beforehand so they had a baseline to measure against during the infusion. The doctor came in and explained that during the infusion there were risks involved, so the nurses would monitor Kristina's vital signs closely, especially for the first 30 minutes. He said the whole procedure generally took about 90 minutes, depending on the patient. He fully expected that once this was done Kristina's red blood counts would come back into normal ranges. They would then monitor her for a period of time to insure the red blood count held and didn't fall again.

It took about 2 hours to complete but the transfusion went without any problems. Kristina and I sat and watched television while the IV added the new blood to Kristina's system. An hour later the phlebotomist took some blood for the lab and we waited hoping everything would be normal now.

The lab work came back in a couple hours and showed Kristina's red blood counts to be in the low/normal range. The nurse said the H&H counts looked good and hoped they would hold stable or increase slightly as the day went along.

CHAPTER THIRTEEN

After a couple days the doctors finally said her blood counts held stable and increased into a more normal range. The doctors said they had nothing more they could do for Kristina and spoke the words she desperately wanted to hear: "You can go home."

I don't think I've ever seen someone's attitude change so quickly when the doctors told the nurses to start the paperwork to discharge Kristina. It isn't hard to imagine how homesick someone can become when they've been in the hospital for several days. She couldn't wait for her own bed and pillow, a home-cooked meal, her family and most of all, I think, a dark quiet room to sleep in without nurses.

We checked out and walked down to the entrance. Kristina and the nurse waited at the door while I went to bring the van down to pick her up. Even then, I felt anxious being separated from her even for those few moments, fearful something might happen that would turned her back around and in a bed again. She was so excited as I helped her into the front seat of the van and we pulled away.

We arrived home shortly after 6:00 p.m. to a hot meal ready on the table. Kristina devoured the light meal then said she felt tired and wanted to go to bed. Her brother, C.J., helped her to her room, setting her bed up and helping her get settled in then they just sat and talked for at least half an hour. You could see how excited he was to have his big sister around again. He spent the evening taking extra care to help Kristina however she needed and just spending time near her.

The next day I went into work feeling hopeful, knowing that I would be going home afterward instead of to the hospital again. After the past several days of the last hospital stay and the many stays over the past weeks I was really getting tired of the cafeteria food and couldn't wait for a meal prepared by my wife. Kristina texted me when she woke up letting me know that everything was good, she was just happy to be able to relax at home finally. She had showered and planned to spend the day writing one of her novels on her laptop, watching her favorite television show, *House, M.D.*, which was on all day.

After dinner we relaxed for a nice evening at home. Kristina still had a lot of chest pain. We tried hard to not make a big deal about it since we were pretty confident by now that it was simply pain and not anything more or related to her heart. The evening plans changed pretty quickly when Kristina told us the pain in her chest had increased dramatically and there was now a shooting pain up through her neck. These were the same symptoms she had presented the last times her potassium levels had increased. Knowing the danger related to elevated potassium we made the decision to head back to the emergency room, just to be safe.

The ride to the emergency room became very tense as the pain increased and Kristina started to black out from the extreme pain. I started wondering if it would be safer to stop and call an ambulance, but knowing that we would easily be at the hospital before an ambulance could arrive I continued on.

Arriving at the hospital, I pulled to the main entrance and quickly jumped out of the van to help Kristina out and into a wheelchair. I hadn't thought about how I would park the van and keep Kristina safe, but those worries were taken care of quickly as the security guard joined us to help me get Kristina into a wheelchair. He then moved her into the emergency room while I drove across the street to park the van. I was back in moments.

The nurses called Kristina into the triage room within minutes, reviewing her vital signs and getting a quick history on her condition. Luckily, her mother, Connie, had had the foresight to put together a list of all Kristina's medications including when she took each prescription during the day. This really helped because Kristina was taking roughly 20 different medications ranging from immunosuppressants to steroids to simply daily vitamin supplements. She also included her dietary restrictions and limitations due to her kidney disease. There is no way I would know what medications she was taking without this list, plus it made it very simple for the nurses to put the information into their system.

They moved Kristina into a room and got her settled into the bed. Of course, as was becoming the routine any time we mentioned Kristina was having that chest pain, the doctors and nurses immediately hooked her up to the EKG monitor. After the past few weeks of steroids and multiple blood draws, the nurses were starting to have a lot of difficulty finding a vein to be able to draw the necessary labs. They put a quick call into the lab and asked that they send a special technician down to Kristina's ER room to help them get the blood samples the doctor had ordered.

Talk about a blessing! The technician who came was a big man, easily 6 feet 4 inches, who appeared to be in his mid-fifties or so. He knew what he was talking about and how to handle a patient. He quietly talked to Kristina, putting her at ease without hiding what he was doing. He quickly found the vein, and before we knew it he had all the tubes full and ready to go to the lab. He explained to Kristina that her veins weren't friendly at all: they curved and bent in strange ways and made it very hard to find a good, straight vein that was large enough to get a needle into and blood out of. He told her what to tell other technicians when they came to draw blood to make things as simple and pain-free as possible, including the needle gauge that would be best to use.

Then we sat and waited. The pain increased, and the doctors offered her some medication to help ease the discomfort. Shortly after, the nurse injected a small dose of morphine through her IV and within a few moments the pain eased slightly and Kristina began to doze off. And we waited. Everything on the EKG monitor looked pretty normal with her heart rhythm and rate, we just need the lab results to come back to make the determination of what to do next. I sat beside Kristina's bed as she slept and offered up prayers for her healing and comfort.

Finally, not long after midnight, the doctor came in a told us the labs had all come back. Her potassium was slightly elevated but within normal limits, and most of the other results were normal. The only result that concerned the doctor was her blood count which was a little lower than normal. The doctor recommended that Kristina be moved to the larger hospital downtown where the doctors were more familiar with her condition and much better equipped to help her out. So, with her permission, the hospital staff began to arrange transport and a room in the other hospital for Kristina.

When we finally arrived and got settled into the new hospital it was nearly 3:00 a.m. Luckily, she was assigned a room in the same wing of the hospital she had just been in, so everything was very familiar, including the nursing staff. We did learn, though, that the doctors had just completed their rotation, so she would have a new team assigned as the primary doctors. Nurse Kelly was between shift rotations, but we knew the nurse on duty. She had Kristina settled in and sleeping comfortably in no time at all. As soon as Kristina fell asleep, I was able to lean back in the chair and get a couple of hours' sleep myself.

The nursing shift changed, and the day nurse on duty was one Kristina had known from her previous stay as well. She was another nurse not much older than Kristina who had a great heart and manner with her patients, at least with Kristina. She took time to sit and talk to Kristina about how she was feeling and to go over her medication list, rearranging the medication in their system to make it as easy as possible for Kristina to take the nearly 40 pills she had to take everyday. She was quick to laugh and seemed to really want to do her best to make Kristina comfortable.

The day went by without anything out of the ordinary, so that evening, not long after Kristina ate her dinner ,I decided to go home, get a shower, and try to get some sleep before going to work the following morning. My long drive home down those dark empty highways was consumed with prayer, as usual. I prayed a lot to God the Father to understand through His decision to send His Son to earth just how I felt about my daughter's present suffering. I prayed hard that God take this away from her and bring her healing. I told God that I couldn't understand what this illness could do to glorify Him. How could a young girl's suffering possibly glorify God? I knew too that our other children were struggling while they watched their oldest sister go through this illness and the near constant hospital visits. Kristina never seemed to be home much, and they were having a lot of difficulty seeing her sick. I started to realize how much a teenager thinks themselves invincible and seeing one so close to their hearts so sick all the time shattered their idea of invincibility.

With this realization, things really came into perspective for her brother and sisters. Some realizations made it difficult to get through their day at school. They couldn't help thinking how trivial some of the complaints their friends voiced were. They felt little sympathy when one would complain that he or she had to take the bus to school today because their mother wouldn't let them take the car.

I was very blessed to be working with several Christian organizations who were always quick to ask about Kristina and offer their prayers. Several of them at their headquarters would take time in their morning prayers to pray specifically for my daughter. Several of the individuals I worked closest with offered their prayers and comfort whenever I would talk to them. They really were a bright spot in my day, and I can honestly say my relationship with each of them became so much deeper in those days that they could never be considered just clients. They were offering their hearts and prayers in our family's time of need. You can never underestimate the meaning of friends like that when times are tough.

I was back at Kristina's room shortly after work again, walking in as she ate a red popsicle and watched one of her shows on the television. She told me the doctors were in earlier and hadn't said that much, but promised they'd be back to speak to me later that evening. Kristina said she had walked around the small circle that made up the unit and had offered prayers for an elderly woman in the room near hers. She told me the woman had no family and was very much alone. Kristina's heart was broken thinking about this woman and how she must have felt. So I promised to bring her a card and small gift the following day.

The nurses required her to get up and walk around the unit as much as she could, telling her that keeping active was the best way to avoid sores and blood clots in her legs. So shortly after Kristina finished her dinner I took a stroll around the unit with Kristina. We couldn't leave the floor area because of the wireless heart monitor she was hooked to, but there was plenty of room to move around within the unit. As we passed a room a man from within cried, we could see a woman sitting there beside his bed, holding his hand. Just guessing from their ages, we both assumed she was his wife. As we passed the room Kristina asked me if we could stop and offer a quick prayer for the man—she hated that he was crying. So together we joined hands and spent a few moments in prayer, asking God to ease the man's suffering.

We continued our walk around the floor stopping in the waiting area. The large windows had a great view of the river and tall buildings that made Pittsburgh's skyline. As we stood gazing out over the city, Kristina turned to me and smiled. She told me that at least she could offer up her ordeal and illness to others in much greater need and suffering. She was glad she could spend some time during the day thinking about and praying for those in the hospital who were truly ill. She didn't consider her illness anything when compared to the other patients in the rooms around hers or in more intense areas of the hospital. She especially felt her heart hurting for all the patients who didn't have someone to come spend time with them and help ease their loneliness—especially the elderly woman a couple of rooms down. She told me how lucky she felt to have a family that cared so much about her and so many people she didn't even know who were praying for her. I told her that all we can do as part of the Church is offer up our suffering to the cross of Christ. , praying that somehow it could be used to help another or in some way to glorify God.

As I stood there looking out through the night at the lit skyline, I couldn't help but think back to that prayer the evening before. How could a young girl's suffering possibly glorify God? Well, that little girl told me how. By being present in the moment, looking for opportunities and "offering it up to the cross," we could make this bad thing into a great blessing. At that time, under the tutelage of my young daughter, I was determined to be the example that she needed to see and for others to draw faith from.

CHAPTER FOURTEEN

As this hospital stay continued, Kristina became very dismayed at the care she was receiving—mostly the fact that the various teams of doctors seemed bent on making her take as many pills as they could. She sat there one evening at dinner and started to cry as she looked at the mound of pills in the small cups in front of her. They were all pills the doctors had wanted her to take with her dinner; she counted 22 different pills for this meal alone.

The doctor came in and sat with her, and between him and the nurse they were able to remove some "extra" medications to treat secondary concerns and rearrange the timing of many to spread the pills out a bit more through the day, so she didn't have so many at one time.

Unfortunately, this stay wasn't a short one. After several days Kristina found herself still in the hospital trying to regulate the high heart rate and still dealing with these blackout episodes that had all the doctors confounded. I'd grown used to them, letting her rest for a period without panic before trying to wake her. It was stressful for me, but I knew now that there didn't seem to be an immediate risk to her health from them, as all the monitors confirmed and history has shown. The nurses were still concerned when an episode occurred—I found myself explaining to any new nurses exactly what could and would probably happen, so they didn't panic and call another condition on my daughter.

At the end of January, the youth minister from our church came into the hospital to spend some time with Kristina. Kristina had been in the youth group since she was a high-school freshman, and I had been a volunteer for just as long. As we sat in the visitor's room, Janet and Kristina talked and laughed about things that were going on. Janet helped Kristina catch up on the news in the youth ministry and high school. Itwas mostly gossip, but that was exactly what Kristina needed at the moment.

Kristina stepped out to run to her room to get something for Janet, and Janet asked how I was holding up. I told her I was doing the best that could be expected. We talked for a bit about what was going on with Kristina's condition, and I guess Janet could tell I was feeling pretty worn out.

Janet asked me if I had considered that Kristina's illness was being used to make a spiritual attack on me. I hadn't really thought about it, but couldn't disagree. Despite all the blessings we've had in the past months, I was feeling cut off and frayed at times. I was often having difficulty finding the words to pray. She asked me if she could pray for me quickly and, of course, I agreed.

After she left, I decided I would redouble my spiritual efforts, just in case I was being attacked.

Saturday, February 5th came—Kristina's 19th birthday. She was still in the same hospital room and still on various monitors, but the day was very bright both with the shining sun and the family, who all came in to help her celebrate this big day and make sure her spirits matched a party atmosphere. She was really uplifted by the many visitors who came in, and the hospital staff was excited to see her so happy. It really was a day that didn't match the venue.

Kristina and the family were uplifted more when the doctor talked about her being more stable and the possibility of going home before too much longer. This probably was the best present she could have received.

Wednesday evening the doctor sat with Kristina and talked to her about her condition. She asked questions, and he gave very truthful answers to this young girl just barely 19. He explained that kidneys don't heal once damaged. So the damage to cells of her kidneys would probably mean that, to help her kidneys remove the fluid from her body, she would at least remain on the water pill, Lasix, for many years, or more likely for the rest of her life. Then Kristina asked the question I think weighed most upon her, "Could I die from this?" And the doctor paused, looking at her and answered that it was a serious condition and she could die from it. But that was why they were working so hard for her to get better. Then he told her that they've come to the conclusion that there was no real reason to keep her much longer, and if everything looked good the next 24 hours or so she could think about going home Friday.

Thursday evening, after a kiss and a prayer goodnight, I left her working on a cross-stitch pattern and went home. I had to work early the next morning and had some meetings, so grandma was going to come out to the hospital early and hopefully bring her home before the day was done.

On my way home I prayed, as I had so many nights before, for her healing. I knew through my prayers and hope that if God so chose He could heal her with a single word, or even just the touch of His tunic. I prayed my Rosary on the drive for Kristina's health, and for my other children and my wife, that we could all have the strength to help Kristina through her challenges and draw closer through everything we were facing. That is what family is about: being there when all others fail, being there in the good and bad. Loving our way along.

As I finished my Rosary, my prayers went back to simply asking God to watch over Kristina again, praying that His will would be to completely wash away this illness and make His glory known through Kristina's healing. But, if not that, then give us wisdom to see Him in all things. But, mostly I think as any father would, I prayed that He heal her.

And, as I pulled onto the final highway I heard God's answer. I heard Him tell me as I prepared to say Amen: "I have to make Kristina sicker so she can be healed. Trust me."

I was really taken aback by those words. They were so powerful and clear. Clear in resonance, but not in meaning. My daughter was scheduled to come home in the morning— what did that voice mean that she would have to get sicker to get better?

The following morning, shortly after 8:00 a.m. my phone rang, my mother on the other side. She told me that I needed to get to the hospital immediately—Kristina had had a seizure and was being rushed to the intensive-care unit. Fifteen minutes later, I was in the hallway outside her room as they prepared her to move to the ICU. My mother explained that she had just arrived and walked into Kristina's room. She said hi and got a smile back from Kristina before Kristina blacked out. The nurse had been in the room as well. But this episode changed everything, because she didn't just black out this time: she had a full seizure. A condition was called again, and the whole hospital rushed to Kristina's room. The doctors medicated and stabilized her. They quickly made the decision that Kristina needed to be moved to the ICU, where she could receive the highest level of care they could provide.

They pulled Kristina's bed from the room to move her to the ICU and stopped so that I could hold her for a moment and give her a kiss. I remember telling her that I loved her deeply and would be with her. I said a quick prayer over her and to her then she was off to the ICU.

My mother and I picked up the various things Kristina had collected over the long hospital stay and prepared to follow her to the ICU. As we stepped into the hallway, the doctor and intern who had taken care of Kristina over the past month's stay came down the hall. The doctor told me again that Kristina had a seizure and was on anti-seizure medication, which is why she was unconscious. They had given her a very high dose to stop the seizure, so it would be hours before she started to wake. He explained that she had vomited during the seizure, and they thought she might have aspirated some, which accounted for her fast and labored breathing. She was being moved because in the ICU the staff could provide Kristina with the highest level of care. The nursing ratio, he explained, was nearly one on one. He comforted me by explaining that the doctors who answered the conditions called on Kristina would now be the ones assigned to watch over and care for her all the time. He felt confident Kristina was in great hands in the ICU, telling me those doctors had seen everything and would do all they could to care for my daughter.

I thanked him. Just as I turned to follow Kristina to the ICU, the doctor took me by the shoulder and told me, "Hold onto your faith. She will be well taken care of." He then looked me in the eye and said that he would be sure to take time throughout the day to offer prayers up for Kristina.

It surprised me at that moment, because he had never mentioned being a man of faith before. But now I could tell in his voice there was no doubt he would be praying for her.

As I walked to the ICU, I thanked God for the strangers he was bringing into our lives who believed God did the real healing. In the elevator, the words from last night came crashing back to me: "I have to make Kristina sicker so she can be healed. Trust me."

By the time we arrived at the ICU, most of our family were already on the way to the hospital. Things were bad, and there was nothing that would keep them from Kristina's side. Within a couple of hours, we had a number of our family surrounding us. Everyone took turns spending time in Kristina's room, since only two at a time were allowed in the room with her. No one knew what to say about what had occurred that morning, but every one of my relatives found some words of comfort that helped keep me calmer.

At dinner the nurse said she was stable. I gave the nurse my cell-phone number, and together we went to a restaurant across the street for a meal. We were gone only a short time, and I was worried that Kristina was alone in that ICU room. But we all needed to eat.

When we were done with dinner and got back to the ICU, I learned my fears of Kristina being alone were unfounded. Our parish's pastoral associate, Dennis, made the drive in to the hospital to see her and spend some time with us all. He had arrived just minutes after we had left to go to the restaurant and because of his position was permitted into her room. Dennis had spent the hour sitting and praying with Kristina.

When we arrived back at the ICU, Dennis took time to sit with us and talk—to lead us in prayer and just provide comfort. He was truly an answer to my prayers. What he did for us can't ever be measured in its impact. His calm demeanor and warm smile were such a comfort. And his simple presence, giving his Friday evening after having worked all day to come and spend time with a girl he didn't really know well and her family, was so meaningful and so Christ-like.

After Dennis had left, I went to Kristina's room and spent some time just sitting with her, praying and talking to her. Though she was still unconscious with the heavy medication, I told her not to worry and just held her hand. I told her that where her room was situated left us in the waiting room on the other side of the wall, just feet away. I assured her that I wouldn't leave.

Before I left her room I asked the nurse if Kristina could have a radio in her room. He said that would be great, and even gave me one to put on the table in the corner. I turned the radio to K-LOVE so Kristina could have music focused on God in the background. I gave Kristina a kiss and left her room, going back to the waiting room while the nurses went through shift change and the associated exams of their patients.

I went out and sat with Connie ,and while we hugged my fears came pouring out. She comforted me by reminding me that God is sovereign and will take care of Kristina. She reminded me of His words to me that He would take care of his daughter.

I knew all of that, but was so afraid of what could happen to Kristina over the next few days. I told her that I believed her words— without doubt I knew that if Kristina closed her eyes here she would open them before Christ, being immediately welcomed home and be forever more joyful. She would be tremendously happy—but that left me without my daughter. She would be in Heaven, but I would be left to mourn and miss her. Though for many years I had prayed "Thy will be done," tonight I couldn't. Tonight all I could think is that I wanted God to heal Kristina and make this all go away.

Connie was such a pillar of faith: while I wavered and struggled she stayed strong, continuing to remind me that we must trust in God, no matter what happened. We were not left alone. He knows what is best for all of us. While we can only see now and worry about later, He has been there and knows everything and the best way for things to work out for His glory. Connie stood up that night in a new light that I will forever cherish.

Within a few hours, the family dispersed and went home. There was nothing to do now but wait and pray.

Shortly after everyone had left, I turned on a computer in the waiting room and sent an email out to my Emmaus brothers, the men who had been so solid in prayer for Kristina since that first day when she was diagnosed. I sent a prayer request for the current situation asking these great prayer warriors to shake the gates of Heaven and make sure God hears her name constantly at His Throne. She needed prayers at this moment and to have the hand of God reach down to take care of her and guide the doctors' thoughts and hands in her treatment. I was so worn and stressed I didn't know where to start with prayers for Kristina, but I knew these men would come through for us.

Shortly later, I was blessed by the first sign of an answer to those prayers. A woman walked into the waiting room, sat down and said hi. Her name was Linda. She told me that morning her 86-year-old mother slipped on some ice and broke her hip. She was in the ICU because her blood pressure had dropped dangerously low. I told Linda about Kristina's situation, I am sure showing my fears and worry about what would happen with her.

Then Linda answered the prayers I had asked from my Emmaus brothers by asking that we take a few moments to pray together for the needs of our loved ones and for strength that we'll need to endure their struggles for them. Her prayer asked God for healing and recovery and for strength and wisdom for each of us that we can show Christ to others around the hospital through these traumatic times.

We sat and talked about our faith and shared stories of Kristina and her mother, finally leaning back in our respective recliners and going to sleep about midnight.

It seemed that I had just fallen asleep when I heard a voice calling my name and touching my shoulder. I woke, groggily, to see a doctor standing beside me. "Mr. Corbett? Kristina is going into respiratory failure. I need to ventilate her right away. Is that OK?"

As he left the waiting room to go back to my daughter's side, I sat up and tried to figure out what he just said. I wanted to immediately run to her room, but held back for a moment to wake myself fully and give the doctor and his team time to do what they needed to care for my daughter.

Just minutes later, I walked into the ICU hallway to see the doctor standing outside Kristina's room. I went over to him and looked into her room. I saw a tube in Kristina's mouth connected to a large machine beside her bed that displayed respiration count, oxygen saturation and other numbers to measure Kristina's breathing. I realized immediately this machine was now breathing for my daughter.

I asked the doctor what had happened. He told me that he believed Kristina had aspirated during her seizure, and that was causing respiratory stress on her throughout the day. Her breathing had been somewhat shallow and rapid all day and had progressively worsened over the past couple of hours. He said that she was in respiratory distress and on the verge of respiratory failure, so he decided the best course of action would be to put her on a ventilator before it became critical. He explained that her breathing was now calmed considerably, as it was being controlled by the machine. She was receiving a medication called fentanyl that kept her fully sedated in a coma-like state.

I asked him what this all means. He said he really couldn't tell me a lot now—only that she seemed stable at the moment but was still highly at risk. He apologized and said that he wasn't completely sure she could make it through the night.

I really felt overwhelmed, as you can imagine, but I thanked him and went into her room. As I sat in the chair next to her bed, holding Kristina's hand, all I could think was that I could lose my daughter. I couldn't let that happen.

I felt so alone. It was 2:15 a.m., and I can't convey how alone I felt at that moment. My thoughts were that I couldn't call anyone to tell them what had happened. I didn't want to wake them. I couldn't think of anything except just how alone I felt at that moment. Everything seemed utterly dark, not in the lighting of the room but in an inner manner. As I look back now I realize how crazy that thought was: with a phone call everyone would have been at our side. But, in my despair, I sat alone in my darkness holding her hand.

After an eternal couple of minutes I pulled Kristina's hand to my head, folding it within my hands. I slid to my knees and cried out to God. I told Him how alone I felt right at that moment and begged Him to keep His promise to take care of His daughter. I poured my heart out in my prayers like I had never done before. I prayed until I had no words left to say; then I knelt there in quiet, holding the hand of the girl who taught me how to love.

Then, through my tears, I heard the same voice I had heard at that retreat a few months back. The strong and warm voice reminded me, "Ed, I told you to trust me. I will take care of my daughter. Just trust in my Divine Mercy."

At that moment a sense of calm and peace unlike I've ever felt before washed over me.

I raised my eyes and glanced around the room. The voice was so real and strong that my first thought was someone had come into the room and was speaking to me. No one was in the room except for Kristina and myself. While looking around, I noticed the clock now read 3:00 a.m. Holding Kristina's hand tighter between my folded hands, with tears rolling down my face, I prayed, "For the promise of Your passion and resurrection I trust in You. Jesus, have mercy on Your daughter."

I envisioned the blood and water from the side of Christ washing over my daughter as I continued to repeat those words, "For the promises of Your passion and resurrection I trust in You. Jesus, have mercy on Your daughter."

I have walked through the dark valley and above I see His cross. The darkness has crushed upon me and over me is His cross. I have feared and run, to find when I feel weak His cross is where I am leaning. That cross shines through, lighting the valley.

And, as I found that February night, when all seems darkest, He is closer. When I seem so alone, He is beside me holding me and giving peace and strength. And I feel His peace.

That February night, at three o'clock in the morning, I learned to trust God and found my faith stronger, at least for the moment. A seed was planted that night, though it would take some time to grow to fruition, and I would face a lot of struggles between then and now.

The following morning, the family returned to the hospital. I updated everyone on the occurrences of the previous night, warning them when they went into Kristina's room they would see her fully sedated on a ventilator that was fully breathing for her. Kristina's brother and sisters were afraid to go to her room. It was impossibly difficult to see their big sister in such a dire circumstance, and terrifying to think of the possible outcomes.

We spent the day rotating visitors to Kristina's bedside. The day was very difficult on everyone. During my rotations with

Kristina I would hold her hand and pray with her as she slept. I reminded her of Christ's promise that everything would be alright and that we simply needed to trust Him. "Everything that happens is to glorify His name. Keep that in mind." I made sure the radio was tuned to the Christian music so she would never feel alone. I don't know if she heard me, but I had read that when someone is unconscious or in a coma, they can hear your words. I made sure every word she heard focused her on the miraculous works Christ would do through her illness.

Late that evening, as the nursing staff was preparing for their shift change routine, I leaned forward to give Kristina a kiss on the cheek, telling her, "I will be right on the other side of the wall, only 20 feet away in the waiting room, and I won't stop praying." I thanked the nurse and told him I would be in the waiting room all night if anything changed. The nurse assured me that he would be there with her so I could get some sleep.

I walked into the waiting room, unable to relax, so I sat and read a book my wife had brought me from home. I looked around the room, noticing only one other man in the room with me. He sat on the other side of the room just staring at the window. I had seen him throughout the late afternoon: he had spent most of the time either in the ICU or sitting alone to the side of the room. He was the kind of person that you didn't really take notice of unless you really looked his way— just very quiet.

I remembered the words I had told Kristina just minutes earlier when I reminded her that God would use her illness to bring glory to His name. That thought brought me out of me chair and led me across the room to the man. I greeted him and introduced myself. He looked my way and told me his name was Michael. He looked very worn and haggard. We spoke for a few moments before I asked the reason he was in the ICU area.

Michael told me the evening before his fiancée was on her way home from work, they were going to go to dinner together. Unfortunately, on a dark and winding section of road a drunk driver coming down the hill and crossed the center line, hitting her vehicle head-on. The other driver walked away with little more than some bruises, but Michael's fiancée had suffered a traumatic head injury in additional to cuts and broken bones. She hadn't woken since the accident and was currently on a ventilator. I told him my daughter was also on a ventilator. Then I did something that was very out of character for me. Normally I would have offered to pray for them and walked away to say a quiet prayer, but this time I found myself asking him if I could pray with him.

He told me that he wasn't too sure about God, but agreed saying that if there is a God that his fiancée needed him now.

So I placed my hand on Michael's shoulder and said a quick prayer asking Christ to send His angels down to be with our loved one in this time of their greatest need. I prayed that He touch these two girls with His healing power and show His powerful glory through them, and that He send His Holy Spirit to give us the strength to bear the days ahead.

When I finished praying, Michael looked up with tears in his eyes and thanked me. We both sat back down and fell asleep for a few hours.

The next morning I woke as the sun came up through the windows of the waiting room. I looked around, noticing Linda had come back during the night and was sleeping in another chair, Michael wasn't in the room. I got up and went out to rinse my face off and get a cup of coffee so I could wake up before being able to get back to my daughter's room.

I entered her room with a smile for her: though she was still sedated and sleeping I wanted everything about my disposition to be positive for her. I sat beside her for a few minutes, saying a quick prayer of thanks for God's allowing her to make it through another night. I felt every hour that passed gave her time to build her strength and heal.

The nurse glanced in and asked how I felt. He told me Kristina had a peaceful night. The nurse asked me if I'd like to stay in the room with her while he woke her. I was perplexed: I didn't know why he would be waking her while she had that tube in her throat and this machine breathing for her. He explained that whenever possible they wanted to wake the patients on a ventilator to do a quick evaluation. She wouldn't fully wake and she probably wouldn't remember anything because of the medications, but she would be awake enough to follow some basic commands for the evaluation. Of course I wanted to be there and see her open her eyes.

The nurse lowered the dosage of the fentaynl being sent through Kristina's IV. After a few minutes he bent over and spoke to Kristina as he gently rubbed her sternum to wake her. Within a few moments her eyes slowly opened, looking at the nurse. When her eyes opened mine filled with tears and I literally had difficulty catching my breath, I was so overjoyed. My mind flashed back to the first time she opened her eyes and looked at me. And then her eyes turned slightly to glance my way, and in those eyes I knew she recognized me. Through the too few moments of the evaluation, whenever he wasn't drawing Kristina's attention to himself, she would turn her eyes to look at me. And every time my heart skipped.

The nurse quickly completed his evaluation and reached over to increase the medication again so she would go back to that deep sleep. Quickly her eyes started to look very heavy again and began to close, but before she was completely asleep again, through my tears, I told Kristina that I loved her deeply and would be right here waiting for her to wake up.

Later that afternoon, the doctor asked me to come back to her room to talk about her situation and their plans. He told me that the plan was to wake her shortly and extubate her, removing her from the ventilator. He explained that over the past several hours they had been lowering the ventilator's assistance giving Kristina the ability to breathe more on her own power. The doctors were now confident that she would be able to breathe on her own. I was excited to hear their confidence.

The doctor and a respiratory nurse came back to the room before too long and said it was time. The nurse lowered the level of the fentaynl slowly, then removed the sedation medication. Within a few moments Kristina started to wake. The doctor told her that he was going to remove the breathing tube but would need her assistance. She nodded, and he told her when he gave the command she should exhale completely. And, as easily and quickly as that, the tube was withdrawn and Kristina was off the ventilator.

Kristina looked around the room, seeming a little confused. Then, seeing me, she smiled.

In a very whispered tone, she asked where she was. The doctor gave her some of the information she was asking while he evaluated her breathing and vital signs. He smiled at both of us and said she seemed strong. He gave her a small suction tube that was reminiscent of one of those suction tubes a dentist might use. The respiratory nurse explained that it was normal for a patient to spit up a lot of fluids after having a breathing tube. This was simply a way for her lungs to start healing and clear themselves to work better. He gave her a small breathing exercise device showing her how to use it. The breathing device was a therapy used to help her lungs recover from the traumatic events and bring them up to full capacity.

Throughout the day Kristina, continued to cough and suction the fluid from her mouth. It was great just having Kristina awake and with us fully again. The family fought for time to be with her and I had trouble just leaving her side. Everyone was so excited to see her recovering and Kristina was happy to see her family there with her, not to mention the stuffed animals and balloons that were around the room.

As the day moved into evening, Kristina's breathing slowly started to become quicker and shallower. The respiratory nurse visited often helping Kristina doing various breathing therapies. During one visit Kristina's doctor motioned me into the hallway. He told me that he was concerned about her breathing, saying that he felt she was progressing back into a respiratory condition. He recommended that they re-intubate her and put her back on the ventilator before the situation became an emergency. My heart dropped but I agreed. While the nurse reset the sedation medication the doctor explained what they were going to do. Kristina looked scared but I assured her that I would be right there with her and bowed my head to hers whispering a quiet prayer into her ear. Then I left the room to let the doctor do what he had to.

After the doctor had left the room I went back to Kristina's side. The nurse told me that one of the effects of the medication that made her sleep was loss of memory. He assured me that she probably wouldn't remember anything of the day so not to worry that it would traumatize her further. The medication would wash it all away.

The next morning was Monday, I needed to go to work. My ex-wife came into the ICU in the morning to let me go home, shower, change and go to the office. I hated leaving her side, but there wasn't much option about work that day. I was confident that the nurse who was with her both days over the weekend would be there while I was at work. He told me he would take care of her for me and let me know immediately if there was any change. So reluctantly I left her side.

The day seemed to go by quickly, and I soon found myself back at the hospital that afternoon. The family all arrived, and we spent the evening visiting Kristina. The ICU doctor told us they were evaluating treatment options and in the morning Kristina would be a focus patient of a group of diagnostic doctors who reviewed the most difficult cases. These doctors were the best the hospital had at diagnosing medical conditions and determining plans.

That evening, the rheumatology team explained that they were recommending a treatment for Kristina to help lower the lupus cell count in her blood. They explained the treatment, called plasmapheresis, would remove the blood from her body through a dialysis-like procedure. As the blood is removed from the body, blood cells and plasma are separated. Her plasma would be collected in a bag, while new, donated plasma was recombined with Kristina's blood cells and put back into her body. The rheumatologist explained to my wife and me that the lupus counts in Kristina's body were extremely high. Since the lupus cells were heavily present in the plasma portion of the blood their hope was that they could lower the lupus counts in her blood by introducing "clean" plasma to her system. They explained the procedure would take place the following morning, starting with the insertion of a dialysis line into Kristina's thigh. The plasmapheresis would then run for several hours. They also said the last lab tests showed Kristina's platelet count was down considerably so when the plasmapheresis was completed if the platelets count didn't rise they would do a platelet transfusion, which was exactly like a blood transfusion simply with platelets instead of red blood.

The plasmapheresis was completed in a few hours, followed by a platelet transfusion and a couple units of red blood as well. While the transfusions were being completed, the ICU team told us that they had done a test when Kristina was re-intubated taking some tissue from the inside of her lungs. The results of the test had just come back showing the cells within her lungs were full of fluid. The Lasix medication simply wasn't enough to help her kidneys overcome the loss of protein and remove the excess fluid from her body. This fluid was then being trapped in her cells. Basically, Kristina was drowning at a cellular level and this would prevent her from being removed from the ventilator until the problem was resolved.

He said this explained a lot of symptoms they've been chasing with Kristina. The fluid accounted for the continued coughing and excessive, continued fluid throughout the day when she had been taken off the ventilator. The extra fluid also was a probably cause of Kristina's increased blood pressure and high heart rate over the past month.

The decision had been made to do another procedure that would help remove the excess fluid from Kristina's body. This procedure, called hemodialysis, would utilize the already present dialysis line in Kristina's thigh. The hemodialysis would have the sole focus of removing the excess fluid from Kristina's body, helping her kidneys catch up. The doctors said the plan was to remove 1,000 ml/hour, continuing until all the extra fluid was removed from her body. I was overwhelmed by how much that sounded like. But the doctors were confident this would put her body back to even ground.

As I stood at Kristina's side waiting for the equipment and technician to come so the hemodialysis could begin, my mind wandered to that prayer in my van just a few nights early when I heard that voice tell me, "I have to make Kristina sicker so she can be healed. Trust me." I dropped to my knees and cried as a lifted my voice to thank God for looking out for Kristina. All of the sudden things came together. The doctors had been chasing her lupus for weeks, unable to find a cause for all the various symptoms she had presented. They were prepared to mark it all up as lupus again and send her home. God, though, knew the reasons and I guess had decided it was time to do more. So she had a seizure, which put her in the ICU and forced the doctors to look at more drastic treatments just to keep her alive. Slowly the root causes were exposed, as one test led the doctors to look at another test until they found the basic reason for her present condition. If God hadn't guided the hands of the doctors, Kristina would have gone home Friday at severe risk. God allowed Kristina to become sicker so the doctors would move past the lupus into the base causes of her critical situation.

When Kristina was brought into the ICU Friday morning, the nurses weighed her at 164 pounds. When the hemodialysis was completed after nearly 28 hours, Kristina weighed only 104 pounds. Without the hemodialysis, her body had failed to expel 60 pounds of fluid. No one knew because she hadn't increased in weight significantly, but instead, as her body was slowly losing true weight, the fluid was increasing, maintaining an appearance of normal weight. we had explained the increase we observed through the past few months as the steroids and her appetite, but it was really the fluid.

Finally, after Kristina had been sedated nearly three days with a ventilator breathing for her, the doctors told us they wanted to be-

gin to wean her off the ventilator with the
goal of soon removing the breathing tube
from her. They started by removing the pressure breathing on the ventilator allowing
Kristina to breathe more on her own power
instead of the ventilator doing all the work for
her. The respiratory nurse monitored
Kristina's assistance. Once the team was
comfortable with Kristina's breathing capacity, the nurse turned off the sedation running
through her IV, and slowly Kristina began to
wake. Her eyes opened and she blinked focusing on her surroundings. She looked at the
doctor as he stood there on the other side of
the bed, listening to her lungs as she took
some shallow breaths. She turned her head
slightly. Seeing me at the foot of the bed, her
face lit up in a smile that deeply touched her
eyes. And once again my heart felt like it
skipped a beat with the excitement of seeing
my baby girl awake again.

The doctor finished his examination, and
with a smile told us Kristina's lungs sounded
clear and everything looked great. Her heart
rate was comfortably within a normal range,
her blood pressure for the first time in a

month was exactly where it should be for her age.

As soon as the doctor left the room I came around the side of Kristina's bed and leaned over her to give her a hug and tell her how much I loved her. To hear her respond telling me "I love you, dad" was one of the greatest moments of my life. My wife just smiled and asked Kristina how she was feeling. Kristina said she felt pretty good but didn't know what was going on or where she was. We sat on separate sides of her bed, each holding one of her hands and explained to Kristina that she was in the ICU. We told her that she had a tough past few days but everything seemed to be improving now.

The respiratory nurse came into the room with a small device that had a tube on one end. The tube seemed to have what appeared to be steam coming out of it. The nurse explained that the "steam" was actually a medication that would help open and heal Kristina's lungs. He explained to Kristina how to use the therapy device and said she would also need to be sure to use the other breathing device he had brought earlier in the week. These breathing therapies were critical in helping her recover from the ventilator. Already in just an hour since waking she was finding less need of the suction tube for coughed fluid.

The next day, the rheumatology team came to check on Kristina. They were very excited that most of her labs were dramatically improved. The lead doctor on the team talked to me in the hallway while they were on their way to the elevator and said how happy he was with the changes over the past few days.

"An older patient would have not handled what she dealt with," he told me. "Her youth saved her."

I could only respond by saying, "Credit youth all you want...I know beyond a doubt the reason she is still with us today. It's all about the prayers that were offered for her. God saved her."

He stopped as the team stepped onto the elevator and looked at me for a moment then smiled and nodded, "No doubt." He stepped back and the doors closed.

CHAPTER FIFTEEN

Just a couple of days after Kristina had the ventilator removed, the doctors told her she would be moved out of the ICU into a regular room. She was doing very well now. They took the next couple hours while they got a room to go through her various medications with the rheumatology team. Her medications were now increased by one, Keppra, to help prevent future seizures. Kristina definitely wasn't pleased with an additional pill to take every day. But her spirits were higher than we'd seen in a long time. She was getting out of the ICU.

The past eleven days seemed like years, but in that short time Kristina had gone from having numerous symptoms for which doctors couldn't come up with a treatment plan to a relatively healthy girl. This Monday morning was a good day that gave a lot of hope again for what the next days might bring.

Tuesday morning I went into the office because my mother and ex-wife were going to spend the day at the hospital with Kristina. They had big plans for the day. After days of being fed through a tube while on the ventilator she could think of nothing she wanted more than a cheeseburger and some fries. So first on the agenda was a visit to the cafeteria. Kristina would get out of her room and get that meal she was craving. After lunch they would take Kristina to the hospital beauty salon to get her hair cut.

They got her a cheeseburger and fries, found a table and pushed Kristina's wheelchair close. She commented that this was one of the best meals she could remember having in a long time. While she sat, slowly eating her meal, she looked up and across the room saw a doctor in his white hospital jacket looking at her. He glanced away then turned his gaze back toward Kristina as he began to walk in her direction. He came up to their table and smiled at her. He said, "Ms. Corbett?"

She nodded, not recognizing the doctor.

He smiled at her and said, "I know you don't remember me, but I was the doctor in the ICU the night you had the seizure. I'm the doctor who put you on the ventilator. I am so happy to see you here."

She smiled and thanked him, not really knowing how to respond.

He continued, "Can I ask something of you? Can you tell me, are you being prayed for?" Kristina looked at him and said, "Yes, my dad told me there are quite a few people who have been praying for me, especially in the last week."

The doctor grinned, "I knew it. I am so happy to see you here like this, because that night I wouldn't have guessed you would be here now eating a cheeseburger. I knew when I saw you from across the cafeteria that there had to be people praying for you, because I did nothing that night. It had to be God." He turned and walked away with a smile.

Early that afternoon my phone rang at work. The nurse from Kristina's floor was calling me, asking if I knew where Kristina was. She had left her room nearly 2 hours earlier to go to lunch but wasn't back yet and the lab was looking for her to take some blood. I told him they had planned to get her hair done after lunch and gave my mother's cell phone number to him so he could call them if he needed them back.

The next day her rheumatology team came in on their daily rounds to check on Kristina. They told her the internists were planning to release Kristina in a couple of days. The doctors wanted her to have a couple days while still in the hospital to work with a physical therapist. She had lost a lot of strength in her muscles during the past week and a half in the ICU. The therapist explained that the fentaynl and ventilator situation typically cause a lot of muscle atrophy. All they could do in a few days was to help her get some balance back and get comfortable walking around the floor some. They could start the process of strength building and help set up a therapist to come to our home when she was released. They'd also recommend an outpatient physical therapy location in our area.

Three days later, we were pulling into our garage. Kristina was very excited to be home after being in the hospital for the past 40 days. I helped Kristina up the two steps into the house and her face lit up when she saw her mom, brother and sisters standing there waiting for her. But most excited of everyone in the house was Buddy, our dog. He walked over to her and sniffed her for a moment— then his tail started wagging vigorously as he recognized her. You could tell he was tremendously excited by the way he leaned into her. He hadn't seen in over a month and obviously had missed her.

Kristina sat to eat her first meal at home in what seemed like forever. She seemed to savor every moment. Before long she was worn out and wanted to go to bed. We found a new challenge: she wasn't strong enough to climb the stairs to her room. We helped her climb the first couple steps before she just couldn't do another. I then lifted her in my arms and carried her up the remaining fifteen steps to the second floor of our house. I gave her a hug, and she walked down the short hallway to her room and slept deeply and peacefully in her own bed and on her own pillow. No nurses to wake her to draw blood or check her vital signs in the middle of the night. No patients in neighboring rooms making noises, no one sharing her room watching television all night. Just simple darkness and quiet bringing blissful sleep.

The next days were great for everyone. Kristina was home so we all got to at home for great home cooked meals each night. No one had late night drives from the hospital. Both my wife and I had to work, and her brother and sisters had school. Since Kristina couldn't handle the stairs on her own we decided that before I would leave for work in the morning, I would wake Kristina early and bring her downstairs to sleep again on the couch. This put her on the main floor, where she had access to a bathroom and could easily get to the kitchen for meals.

The home health nurse came the fourth day home. She spent time just sitting with Kristina, getting to know her. She explained that she would visit every two to three days to check Kristina and draw some blood for labs ordered by the doctors.

The physical therapist came the next day. He evaluated the house for Kristina's therapy needs and plan focus. He told her that an outpatient therapy center would be better able to provide the best therapy for her, but that he could get her built up. While they worked through her first day of therapy exercises they talked about themselves. Kristina found out that Dave was a parishioner of our church. Little things like that can help so much to make one comfortable.

The next day our new pastor, Father Bob, called the house. He had only come to the parish a week earlier, but had heard about Kristina from the staff at in the church's office. He asked if he could stop by to meet Kristina, bringing her communion. When he arrived my wife and I left the room to give them time to talk. Father Bob has a very comfortable and warm personality. They talked for an hour. He is such a great shepherd, a new pastor caring for his new flock. When he left the house, we could see how visibly uplifted Kristina was. He had done a great job listening to Kristina and then giving her some spiritual healing in his response.

Later that week I purchased a new iPod to hold the music I listened to on my ride to work. I hadn't owned one before, so didn't know much about apps or other functions it could do. I went into the App Store just to see what was available, finding myself within just minutes looking at an app called, "Divine

Mercy." The app was free so I downloaded it. I spent the next days totally engrossed by what this app contained. I found myself reading the story of a saint I had never heard of before, but with whom I felt a connection for some reason. As I read the story of the life of St. Faustina I became enthralled and thought of purchasing her Diary. —though I wasn't sure —could reading a diary really be exciting?.

I also found a prayer in this app that took my breath away. I couldn't believe what I was reading as I read through the Chaplet of Divine Mercy. The words brought me back to that Friday night just weeks ago in the ICU with Kristina on the ventilator. When I was feeling so alone that night, the words came back like a lightning bolt: "For the promises of Your passion and resurrection I trust in You. Jesus, have mercy on Your daughter." I looked down at the words of the Chaplet to find my words that night before me, "For the sake of His sorrowful passion, have mercy on us and on the whole world."

And then there was the picture of Jesus front and center to St. Faustina emblazoned with the words, "Jesus I trust in you."

CHAPTER SIXTEEN

Two weeks after Kristina came home she was still home and having few problems. She still couldn't climb the stairs without a lot of help. The pain in her chest was still present but manageable if Kristina stayed well rested.

The couples Bible study group my wife and I belonged to had a monthly get together scheduled. Connie and I were excited to go see our friends and spend some time out together. We hadn't been part of the group for the past four months since we had spend most Saturdays in the hospital since December. Four months after Kristina's first hospital stay caused by the high potassium, we were able to get together with the same friend who had come during his rounds to visit her and lift us up.

While we stood around the kitchen island enjoying the fine food prepared by our hosts, Connie and I updated everyone on Kristina's past few weeks. We found ourselves telling them of Kristina's visit from Christ in the emergency room two months earlier. Everyone, including our friend Father Sam, listened closely, hanging on to every word. Then we got to the Friday Kristina had that seizure and the happenings in the ICU. I told them how I had heard that voice telling me that Kristina had to become sicker so she could get better. We told them of the miraculous healing that had taken place and the doctor's words about how he had nothing to do with Kristina's healing.

When we had finished telling of all events of the past months one friend looked at me and said, "Wow, your faith was so strong through everything. What would you have done if things would have turned out differently Friday night?"

That question really stopped me in my tracks. I knew how my faith was challenged that night, remembering my words to Connie. I couldn't forget my despair that though Kristina would have been with Christ that night, I would have been left alone without her. But I also couldn't forget how that evening I felt trust in God's promise that He would take care of His daughter.

It is hard to explain all the thoughts that raced through my mind in those few moments. The only response I could think of was that all I would have had would have been my faith. As the thought lingered, I couldn't help thinking of the lie that answer had been. I wondered deep inside if I would have kept my faith if things had gone another way that night in the ICU.

The following week, I went to help out with our teen group at church. As the kids talked about the topic of the night, I leaned against a shelf in the library. Glancing to the shelf I noticed a book that was leaning against the others but with its cover facing me. I was stunned to see the diary of St. Faustina, *Divine Mercy in My Soul*. I instantly took it from the shelf and checked it out of the library. It took me less than an hour when I got home to know I needed to purchase a copy of this book for myself.

The next few weeks, life returned to a more normal routine. The therapist and nurse each came three times a week. Kristina's strength slowly increased and a month after her last hospital stay she climbed the stairs to her bedroom for the first time. It was such an exciting accomplishment that added hope of a return to normalcy.

A new clinic opened very close to our home, listing a rheumatologist who specialized in lupus. This was great because the new clinic was a 10-minute drive from our house as opposed to the rheumatologist in the other system that was more than an hour's drive. I mentioned the doctor to my mother. She knew this doctor was associated with the Lupus Center in West Penn Hospital, which was led by a doctor considered to be one of the most respected lupus specialists in the country.

Kristina transferred to these new doctors, who immediately showed their level of knowledge and expertise regarding lupus. The level of care was dramatically different. Her new doctor sat at each appointment to simply talk to her about how she was feeling. He would examine her in depth at every appointment, spending time to help her understand her condition and what his plans for treatment were.

Unfortunately, Kristina's struggles weren't over yet. Early one August evening the chest pains returned strong enough that we were forced to take Kristina back to the emergency room. The doctors did their normal labs and found her heart enzymes elevated. They were concerned again about a possible heart attack, so again they decided it would be best to transport her to the larger hospitals downtown. This time, though, we went to Allegheny General Hospital in Pittsburgh, because her new rheumatologist was there.

The following day the cardiologist decided there was enough evidence in the still-increased heart enzymes and some reading from the EKG to warrant doing a heart catherization to check her heart for any blockages or abnormalities. The doctors were concerned because they said lupus could cause heart tissue damage or a thickening of her blood that could result in blockage.

While they prepared to move Kristina to the cath lab for the procedure, Kristina blacked out. There were no other symptoms present, just unconscious, but the doctors ordered an EEG anyway. While we waiting for the technician to come to perform the EEG,

Kristina woke up. The EEG found nothing, so the following day the cardiologist performed the heart catherization. This test came back negative as well. There was nothing found within her heart that would be cause for the chest pains. The following day Kristina was on her way home.

A few days later while sitting on the couch watching television, Kristina blacked out. This time, though, it changed dramatically. Shortly after Kristina blacked out she started screaming in pain. Connie and I were at her side trying to calm her down, but every time we touched her she would simply swat at our hands and scream louder. Not knowing what else to do we called 911 to get an ambulance to our house. A police officer arrived first, followed within minutes by the ambulance and paramedics. The paramedics came into the house as we updated them on the reason for their presence. Kristina, still lying on the couch, continued to scream in pain. The paramedics had difficulty evaluating Kristina because every touch brought more pain and screaming from Kristina. They carefully laid her on their stretcher, then loaded her in the back of the ambulance. I ran to the garage and followed quickly after the ambulance as it left for the emergency room.

When I arrived at the emergency room, Kristina was already settled into a treatment room. I gave the nurse Kristina's list of medication and sat down waiting for the doctors. Within a few hours the doctors decided again to transfer Kristina downtown to the larger hospital. Her new rheumatologist was linked to Allegheny General Hospital so the emergency room worked to get Kristina into a room.

The stay at AGH was typical of most early visits to the hospital. The doctors ordered blood work, and we sat and waited. The doctors couldn't determine any reason for the pain and fell back to diagnosing the blackout as a pseudo-seizure. We spent two days in the hospital before the doctors released Kristina.

Two days later, Kristina blacked out at home and another episode of pain and screaming ensued. Connie and I spent over an hour trying to calm Kristina before we decided that we had no choice but to call for an ambulance again. The same paramedics arrived this evening. They walked in calmly, asking if anything was determined the last time they had transported Kristina to the emergency room. We updated the paramedics on what the doctors had said as they prepared Kristina to be taken back to the emergency room. Again the paramedics took Kristina to the emergency room, and again she was transferred and admitted at AGH downtown. The pain was considerable.

This time the doctors diagnosed the pain as neuropathy, adding a new medication to Kristina's list. They hoped the new medication would counteract the extreme pain. The doctors ordered another EEG in an effort to determine a cause for the continued blackouts. The EEG showed nothing of note despite the fact that Kristina blacked out during the test. Again, within a couple days, Kristina was released without any resolution to her conditions.

Over the next weeks, every evening Kristina would suffer from an extreme pain episode and quickly black out. Connie and I spent the nights trying to help Kristina through these episodes. We knew the ambulance and emergency room would be able to do nothing for her, so we did our best to comfort her and get her to wake up. Typically when Kristina would wake she would have little memory of the episode, feeling some residual pain and being very tired. Many nights were spent sitting beside her bed or the couch while she suffered through hours screaming in pain unable to be awakened. There was nothing we could do but try to comfort or console her. The best we could find was to sit with her, talking to her and using cold compresses on her forehead. These small things gave her some comfort, or at least no additional pain, giving us some illusion that we were helping her through the episodes.

One evening we were able to get her to wake for a short while, only to have her angry response directed at us. She was upset because she said she had seen people who had invited her to stay with them. She didn't recognize the people or really remember too much about them, only that they were telling her to stay with them—they would make her better and take away her illness. She woke, as always, very tired, with that same residual pain that she would describe as feeling like her nerves were on fire.

The visits from the people from her "dream" continued often from that point.

Kristina would sometimes remark about their presence, always with the same feelings towards them. She would feel like she didn't want to wake and leave them. We tried to talk to her and figure out who they were, but never were able to get past those vague feelings. She felt safe with them and found it really difficult to leave and wake up.

I had started the process at work to transition from working at the office to working in my home office. This really gave us a lot of comfort. Though every episode would occur in the evening, just being there with Kristina and knowing she was OK during the day would take a lot of stress off everyone.

The episodes of extreme pain continued almost every night, and by early November we were at our wit's end. Several nights every week were spent in the emergency room waiting for doctors to tell us again that nothing showed on any labs or other tests that they could treat with anything more than some morphine to help ease her pain and suffering. The doctors prescribed Oxycontin and Oxycodone for her to take at home in hopes of easing the pain. Nothing seemed to make the pain go away. At best, the medications only took some of the edge off the pain for Kristina. Even with all the labs and doctors and medications, the blackouts continued nightly and were always accompanied by severe pain and fits of screaming.

Sleep was a difficult thing for Connie and me to find. We would spend hours each evening with cold and warm compresses, trying to provide any comfort we could to Kristina. Connie would sit beside her, gently rubbing her back in an effort to calm her—somehow, even though it seemed that just an air movement on Kristina would set her nerves on fire, Connie's touch didn't make Kristina's pain increase, and actually seemed to help for short periods of time. Some nights we would carry her to her bed, while other nights she stayed on the couch in her pain. I would kneel beside her for hours praying my Rosary in the dark night. Many nights I slept on the floor beside Kristina, trying to provide any comfort I could while she often moaned and tremulously shook.

We found a Christian counselor to visit, hoping she would be able to help Kristina through whatever psychological problems there might be behind her pain episodes. The counselor understood the way the spirit and soul influenced one's physical and mental wellness.

Unfortunately, we had little luck with Kristina spending a lot of time with the counselor. The first time at her office, as we sat in the waiting room Kristina had another of her episodes. She blacked out sitting in the waiting-room chair, then quickly started groaning in pain. Before long Kristina was screaming in pain. The commotion disrupted the counselor's session with her current patient. The counselor ended that session and then, when we were the only ones remaining in the office, knelt down to try to help Kristina calm. She told us it seemed almost like there was some other influence causing this episode to occur, but wasn't sure what that cause might be. But whatever the cause it was very powerful.

Unfortunately, from that attempted visit on, most visits to her office involved Kristina blacking out and falling into her pain episode. Rarely did they have time to sit and talk. On those rare occasions they were able to speak, the counselor was able to pull together some thoughts and highly recommended we visit our chiropractor. She said he was skilled in some techniques that could help calm Kristina's nervous system. The counselor felt strongly that everything Kristina had gone through in the past months had thrown her neurological system out of balance. The fact that Kristina had become so sick so quickly had take her body into such deep illness that her mind couldn't catch up. And when the neurological system started to recognize the illness within her system, Kristina started to recover from the deepest effects of the lupus, only to have her mind telling her she was sick with her body in disagreement.

Within a few days we were in our chiropractor's office. He sat and talked to Kristina and did some treatments on her. He didn't find anything too out of the ordinary, especially for a young girl who had been so ill.

While I was talking to the chiropractor, Kristina blacked out and started to moan in pain. Dr. Maury moved to her side and checked her breathing, evaluating her current symptoms. He then leaned her forward slightly in the chair and moved his fingers down her spine. With a few pops of his manipulation device, in fact just a small pen-like instrument that gave a slight and painless snap, Kristina's eyes opened and the pain edged away. He talked to Kristina for a few moments to make sure she was OK, and then explained what he thought was happening. First, he said, it was beneficial that this episode occurred while she was in his office. He was confident that Kristina's neurologic system was really out of sync. He explained that in most people this exhibits itself in hyperactivity, resulting in racing heart and breathing. But Kristina's system was reacting in the opposite manner. Her system was dealing with the trauma she'd gone through over the past months by simply shutting itself down. He recommended continued visits so he could work to realign her nervous system and that she start immediately doing biofeedback.

He recommended a device that would help her do the biofeedback at home. It simply helped her focus on controlling her breathing, with a light that would register a red color if her pulse and breathing weren't balanced with the device. The lights would turn green if everything was in synchronization.

Kristina ordered the device, and three days later it arrived in the mail. No matter how hard Kristina tried she couldn't get the biofeedback device to register anything but a red light. Connie and Christopher tested it out to find that with no effort at all they could keep it in the green. So I tried. And the device would start in the red and over a few minutes would slowly move into the green.

I watched Kristina work at this a few times each day for the next weeks, slowly seeing some progress as the device started to at least move into a bluish-green tint. As I would work with her, I thought this rhythmic bio-feedback was very reminiscent of praying the Rosary. The rhythm and repetition was so calming, helping both breathing and heart rate calm but also giving a sense of peace about the mind at well. I mentioned this thought to our chiropractor during the next visit. He agreed, saying the monks of old may have been some of the first to recognize biofeedback, though they didn't know it at the time. Prayer in itself can have a calming effect on a person, and adding the rhythm made it balancing to the mind and body.

CHAPTER SEVENTEEN

None of the medical doctors had a solution, but not one of them contested what our chiropractor had said about Kristina's nervous system. They agreed, saying there was probably a lot of truth to this, somewhat like a physical post-traumatic stress syndrome. They recommended Kristina visit a counselor to help her deal with all she had been through in the past year.

We found a therapist nearby who focused in prayerful, Christian counseling techniques. Kristina and the counselor would spend time a few times each week together. The counselor did find a lot of stress and fears within Kristina. The extremes and frequency of Kristina's episodes started to lessen somewhat over time.

With all that had occurred over the past year, the ups and downs that lifted my family up and brought us to our knees, the past few months had been the hardest by far. We were in a sense locked within our house, trying to administer aid to Kristina with no knowledge of what to do to make things better for her. The nights seemed at times eternal when she was blacked out, and especially when the pain came on her. In those nights time seemed to stop, and the night became so much darker.

While nearly all of Kristina's episodes occurred at night, the days were just as difficult at times because of the ever-present stress and lack of a real night's rest. Knowing Kristina was home while we were at work added to the fears. If she didn't answer the phone right away, the thoughts could run away.

One morning I talked to Kristina. for a few minutes—she had just woken up and said she was going to go down to the kitchen, get some breakfast, and then relax and write a short story while watching television. A couple of hours later I called her cell phone—no answer. So I called the home phone, and again no answer. I tried several times, and with each attempt my concerns grew. I finally made it home when my day was done at the office. I came through the door from the garage, and my first thought was how strange it was that Buddy wasn't waiting at the door as he usually did. I walked into the kitchen, and there in the hallway was Kristina lying face down on the floor. Buddy was snuggled up to her side looking at me. I ran to her. She was uninjured but unconscious. I lifted her and carried her to the couch in our living room. She woke an hour later and told me that the last she remembered was walking toward the kitchen to eat breakfast.

As the stresses continued I started to struggle with my prayers. The prayers weren't coming as easily as they had over those months when Kristina had been in the hospital so much. My focus during the day wasn't there. I found it very difficult to keep my mind on my readings from the Bible, and soon found myself not reading it at all.

As the weeks passed, just going to Mass each Sunday felt more like a chore. I thought of excuses to stay home and rest, but because my wife was always ready to go I couldn't let her know my desire to miss just once.

November came, and I was asked by our youth minister if I would consider being an adult chaperone for the annual teen retreat again. I really didn't feel the energy to attend this year, but our youth minister begged me to attend since they were short of male chaperones for the parish group attending. This year my son was going on retreat, too, so I finally relented and agreed to go.

The retreat was uneventful. As usual, the teens were very energetic, never seeming to sit down to relax.

Saturday afternoon came, and time for a break from the talks and events. The teens had a couple of hours to unwind and play. As a chaperone I was tasked to float around the main grounds of the retreat center to make sure the teens were staying safe and not misbehaving.

I stood by the cafeteria patio watching some teens play a game of soccer with some visiting religious sisters from Steubenville. It was great to see the sisters have so much fun. They way they interacted with the teens set such a great example, showing that they could give their lives fully to God but still be just girls at heart. To see the sisters and teens laughing and giving high fives when one scored a goal was incredibly uplifting.

Standing not far off, I noticed, was one of the priests who were at the retreat for the day to give some talks to the teens. Father Joe was a young, new priest not long out of seminary. He is an incredibly prayerful and spiritual man.

I had failed to go to the Sacrament of Reconciliation the day before as I traditionally did before a retreat. Looking at Father Joe standing there, I thought to ask if he would take a few moments to hear my confession. So I walked over, and as I asked him to hear my confession I noticed a few boys pulling out a football. Father Joe before joining the seminary and ultimately being ordained as a priest had been the starting quarterback for the University of Buffalo. I've heard that he stood a decent chance of being drafted into the NFL before he felt his calling to the priesthood. I suddenly felt bad because I knew he would want to play some football with the boys, so I told him that my confession would be short.

So I began, making the sign of the cross and saying the words "Forgive my Father, for I have sinned...."

I made a quick listing of the sins that were weighing on my mind, to be honest, nothing more than I would list most times. I figured I'd give my quick list of sins, Father would say some words and give the absolution through Christ's power of forgiveness and he'd be off to play some touch football.

Things didn't go quite as planned, though. Father Joe really shocked me when I was done as he looked at me for a few moments before saying, "Ed, you are really having a problem with trusting God, aren't you?"

"What? No, I trust God."

"No, you are struggling now to believe God works everything for the good, and that is leading you to struggle with trust in Jesus Christ, isn't it?"

For the next hour Father Joe talked to me about where I was. As he spoke I realized the words he was saying were right on the mark. And as he stopped to say another prayer over me, I realized that my prayer from the past year had trapped me. I realized that when I told God that I couldn't give my daughter over to His will, I had started myself on a path to lose all trust in God.

Father Joe told me of struggles he had in his life and how he always had to work to keep his heart and mind focused on trusting God. He told me how his brother had passed away years earlier and the struggles with his faith that had caused. Father Joe explained to me that he would often lie awake at night in his bed and hold the Crucifix against his chest. He would focus his thoughts on the cross and Christ's sacrifice and then repeat over and over, "Jesus I trust in You...Jesus, I trust in You."

And I could feel my heart breaking with those words, "Jesus I trust in You."

St. Faustina interceded for Kristina that night in the ICU. She had pursued me through the past months, showing up in various unexpected ways, slowly delivering her message to trust Jesus. And now I felt she was directly interceding for me in my hardness.

And as I listened to her words of Christ's love and mercy come from this priest, I felt the darkness start to subside and fall away. I broke down crying as Father Joe settled his hands on my head and gave me the forgiveness of Christ through the power of the Church. I could feel a warmth of love flow through my body as those words were spoken by Father Joe, telling me that God loves me and forgives my weaknesses and failures of the past months.

That evening, as I lay awake, listening to the boys joke in the other room, I looked at the app on my iPod and was further consoled by what I read from paragraph 1602 of St. Faustina's diary. "When you approach the confessional, know this: That I Myself am waiting there for you. I am only hidden by the priest, but I Myself act in your soul."

And there in the darkness, with the other male adult chaperones fast asleep in their beds, I thought about how far I had wandered from God in the past couple of months. I hadn't even realized it was happening, but now in retrospect I could see how far I had slipped away. I began to weep.

The following week, after the retreat ended, I received a call from an Emmaus brother, Jim. He asked me how Kristina was doing, and we talked for a while about everything that was happening in each other's life.

Jim then stopped and said, "Ed, I've been asked to lead the next Emmaus retreat in April. I've been praying about the team and would like to ask you if you would be willing to serve on the team during the retreat."

I immediately said I would, but quickly thought I had better check with my wife before giving my commitment. So I asked Jim to hold a moment while I talked to Connie. I told her about Jim's invitation to serve on his retreat team in April and asked if she was OK with me agreeing. She quickly responded that she didn't see any problems. I told Jim I was very humbled by his invitation and would be honored serve in any way he asked.

I went back to the other room and thanked Connie for being so supportive and allowing me to serve on the Emmaus retreat team. She told me she had been praying the past few days that God would do something to help me. It had become clear to her over the past couple of weeks that I was really struggling with my faith. At first she thought it was mostly because of the stress and lack of a good night's sleep, but in the past days she had started to see more clearly that my faith was shaken. She reminded me that I always

needed to trust God and remember His promise that night in January that everything will
be OK if we simply trust Him. This invitation,
she felt, was an answer to her prayers. She
understood how much the Emmaus ministry
meant to me and how much the men of the
ministry had done to help us through the last
year of our life. She knew that being involved
with this retreat and being around my Christian brothers would help lift me back up.

A few weeks later, Jim, the retreat team
leader, called me. He told me that he had
been praying about the various talks during
the weekend and felt strongly that I should
give a talk about trusting God.

I was surprised that of all the talks that
took place on the weekend he would ask me to
give this one. Everything Father Joe told me
and that I'd been experiencing over the past
weeks started to really become clear. God
knew I was having a problem trusting Him at
the moment, and that lack of trust was leading me down through a dark night. But He
was giving me the opportunity to start trusting again. As my Emmaus brothers always
jokingly said, "He was using the 2x4 to our
head to get our attention."

As January came Kristina's episodes continued. Though the episodes weren't as severe as they had been the past several months, they still occurred most nights. One night, feeling desperate, I put a crucifix on a rope necklace over Kristina's bedpost along with a blessed medal of St. Benedict the Abbot. St. Benedict the Abbot's medal is famous for exorcism and protection from evil. And starting that evening Kristina seemed to be able to sleep in her bed a bit more peacefully.

But she still seemed to be in bad shape. Many times when Kristina would black out now we couldn't wake her no matter how much we tried. She would often remain unconscious for hours.

CHAPTER EIGHTEEN

Sunday, January 22nd, Connie and I woke early. We ate breakfast, thinking we would give Kristina a few more minutes of sleep before we woke her to start getting ready to go to church as well.

We finished breakfast but still hadn't heard Kristina getting ready yet so I went up to her room to wake her and get her moving. When I tried to wake her I could tell she was having one of her blackout episodes. I said her name a few times then gently tried to shake her awake. But nothing I did seemed to make her wake, and I actually seemed to be causing Kristina some discomfort. I called Connie, and together we tried to wake Kristina. Again, nothing we tried seem to make any difference. We decided to give her a little more time before trying again.

After about thirty minutes of checking on her we tried further to wake her. Connie put a cool compress on her forehead as she sat beside her on the bed. We discussed what we would do about getting to Mass if Kristina didn't wake up soon. At this time we would be hard-pressed to make it together even if she woke right away. I was serving at the 10:00 a.m. Mass as an Extraordinary Minister of Holy Communion so thought that I would go to the early Mass while Connie stayed with Kristina; then later in the afternoon Connie would attend at a neighboring parish.

As I was preparing to leave Kristina started to moan, appearing to be in some pain. We were beginning to become concerned that she might fall into a full episode, so I decided that it would be safer if I stayed home with Connie to watch over Kristina. For the next ninety minutes we continued to attempt to wake Kristina, all the time trying to keep her as comfortable as possible to avoid her falling into more pain. we wanted to avoid the stress those episodes caused to us as well as to Kristina as much as possible—not that we really had a choice if it began, since we'd never really figured any way to stop them once they start.

Finally, Kristina's eyelids fluttered and she started to slowly wake up. A few more minutes and her eyes opened. We asked her how she was feeling. She looked around the room appearing to be a little confused. After a moment she looked at us and said, "Who are you? Where am I?"

We were startled by the question. Connie replied, "Kristina, you're in your room. We're mom and dad, remember?"

Kristina looked at her for a moment then replied, "No. Am I Kristina?" "Yes."

I helped her sit up as Connie held her hand. She looked around the room and now we recognized the look on her face. She was lost. She had no idea who or where she was. She didn't recognize us or the surroundings that should have been so familiar.

Panic started to set in for both of us. We decided if things didn't change really fast we would need to get her to the hospital.

Kristina commented that she felt strange and rubbed her stomach. She said it felt empty. I told her she was probably hungry and asked if she wanted something to eat.

She shrugged. So, while Connie helped Kristina out of her pajamas into a shirt and some jeans I went to the kitchen to prepare some soup for Kristina.

A few minutes later Kristina was seated at the kitchen table still looking around the room trying to figure out where she was. I sat the bowl and a spoon in front of her but all she did was stare at it. So, I lifted the spoon as stirred the soup for a moment telling her to eat. She grabbed the spoon and slowly stirred the contents of the bowl, mimicking what I had just done. I realized she didn't know how to eat. I showed her what to do and while she sipped the broth from the bowl, Connie and I started preparing to leave the house to take Kristina to the emergency room.

Kristina commented that her stomach felt funny. We questioned her to determine what she meant by the comment. After a few minutes we determined that she had to use the restroom. She didn't even remember how to do that. Connie helped her to the restroom while I grabbed Kristina's shoes and the van keys so we could leave. We loaded Kristina into the van and pulled out of the driveway a few minutes later.

I watched Kristina in the rearview mirror, and Connie continually turned to check on her. She simply sat in her seat and quietly looked out the window or around the interior of the van, an empty look on her face.

About halfway between our house and the hospital Kristina said, "Do you know Jesus is nice?" Connie replied, "Of course."

Kristina said, "Jesus has brown hair."

Connie looked back and asked, "Really? How do you know that?" Kristina's response nearly caused me to have wreak the van, "He is sitting right here. Don't you see Him?"

Connie nearly turned out of her seat looking back and my head turned to see what she was talking about. Maybe we both had the hope that we would see Jesus sitting in the back seat with Kristina.

Unfortunately, we didn't see anything, but we could both tell Kristina was looking at something or someone. The confused look on her face seemed to ease somewhat.

We asked Kristina if he had just appeared. She told us, "No, He was with me at the house when I was sitting at the table eating. When you gave me the soup."

As we pulled into the drive heading up toward the hospital and the emergency room, Kristina said, "Jesus said He will take care of everything if I just trust Him."

Connie replied, "You should always trust Jesus, He is God and knows the best for everything all the time."

Kristina smiled at her and said, "He said I should listen to you because you are exactly right."

I parked the van and then helped Kristina to the emergency room. A nurse met us as soon as the security guard checked us in. She took us back to an observation room. I stepped out while Connie helped Kristina put on a hospital gown. The nurse then began to check Kristina in, verifying all her medications as well as the reason for our visit.

The nurse then put a IV in Kristina's arm and drew some blood for the labs the doctor had ordered. Then we sat waiting for the doctor to come evaluate Kristina and hopefully give us some idea what was going on.

Connie and I sat on the opposite side of the bed from the door. When the doctor and nurse left the room, Connie asked Kristina if Jesus was still there in the room. Kristina looked up, pointed toward the door and said, "He is right there." She continued, "Jesus says He is going to help me to remember things."

We told her to ask Him what our names are. Kristina glanced at the door and said, "He said your name is Ed, you're my dad, and your name is Connie, you're my mom."

Stunned, we both stared at the door. Neither of us knew what to say as we both looked at her then each other in disbelief. Or maybe it wasn't disbelief—it might have been a point where we were both starting to really believe.

We asked her again if Jesus was still in the room with us.

Kristina told us, "No, he had to leave to help other people. But He told me not to be afraid. He wouldn't leave me alone."

Just as she finished saying that, the doctor walked into the room to examine Kristina. He asked several questions and completed his examination. We explained what had occurred earlier that morning: how we had difficulty waking her, and then when she did wake, it was with no memory at all. He spoke for a few moments then left the room, telling us he'd come back once they had labs and knew what they were going to do.

We sat quietly for the next hour or so waiting. Kristina dozed off, taking a short nap. As we sat there for the next hour, Connie and I had a lot to think about in the silence.

The doctor finally returned and said all the labs looked pretty good, except that one of the indicators noted some inflammation in Kristina's system that could be caused by her lupus. He told us they were recommending transferring Kristina downtown to Allegheny General, where the rheumatologists were better equipped to handle the lupus and where they would be able to have the staff psychiatrist evaluate Kristina.

Connie and I decided that, when the ambulance left to take Kristina downtown, I would take Connie home before following Kristina to Allegheny General. Connie would take care of the other kids and our dog.

It took another hour while the staff arranged a room at Allegheny General and called the ambulance to transport her. As the paramedics loaded Kristina on the stretcher for the ambulance she looked at us and said, "Don't worry, I'll see you there."

I took Connie home then drove downtown. This gave enough time for the ambulance to get Kristina to the hospital and for the staff of Allegheny General to check her into the room and get her settled. They always did their initial evaluations as soon as she arrived.

I got to her room within thirty minutes of her arrival. The nurse assistant was in the room with her telling her how to use the call button on the bed if she needed anything. She demonstrated how to use the bed and pointed out the television controller. I asked when the doctors would be in to evaluate her. The nurse told me the doctors would probably be in shortly, but she couldn't say exactly when they'd arrive.

So again we sat down to wait. Kristina relaxed for a little bit, then looked at me and told me that Jesus had been with her in the ambulance during the whole ride, but she didn't think the paramedics knew He was there. She said He told her that He was there to take care of her only and that no one else needed to see Him. She then surprised me again when she told me that Jesus had told her what her address and phone number were as well as the name of her aunts and her grandmother, my mother.

As she told me these things, I received a text message from my sister who lives in Florida. She told me mom had called to tell her Kristina was in the hospital again and that they were all praying for her.

When the doctors finally came, they did a short evaluation then talked to Kristina, gauging her current condition and memory. She barely remembered anything except for the things she said that Jesus told her. As the doctors left the room I followed them into the hallway to ask what the plan was and what they thought might be going on. They told me that honestly at this time they didn't know what had caused her loss of memory, but their first plans were to have the rheumatologist and a psychiatrist visit her for further evaluations.

As they turned to walk away I looked down the hallway to see one of my Emmaus brothers walking toward me. He was dressed in scrubs. I knew Andy was a nurse, but had no idea that he worked at Allegheny General.

We talked for a few minutes before he asked if it would be all right if he went into

Kristina's room to say hello to her. They talked for only a few minutes before Andy asked if he could pray with Kristina. She smiled and agreed. He said a short prayer asking God to continue to watch over Kristina and to help her recover so she could go back home as soon as possible.

After Andy left the room to go back to his floor, I sat in the chair and Kristina napped. I had grabbed my Bible when I dropped Connie off at the house, so I sat there and stared absently at the words on the page, unable to really concentrate enough to read. I looked at Kristina and prayed. As well as asking for Kristina's healing, I asked God to help give me strength to get through this day and this event.

I looked down at my Bible and saw the verse from 2 Corinthians 12:9 highlighted on the page in front of me—"But He said to me, 'My Grace is sufficient for you, for My power is made perfect in weakness.'"

As I sat there contemplating what this verse meant to me at this time, a thought came to my mind. People always say that God gives enough strength to get through the day or through your struggle, but sitting there looking at those words from 2 Corinthians 12:9, I suddenly knew that God doesn't give strength to get through the day, He gives exactly enough grace and strength to deal with the present moment and again for the next moment. The realization came upon me that while Jesus is the Alpha and the Omega, He is "I AM" the God of the present moment. He knows the beginning and the end of the story, and with that He is present in the moment, giving us exactly what we need to carry on, making His strength perfect. I was overwhelmed with this revelation and sat there crying as I watched Kristina sleep.

Late that night I kissed Kristina on the cheek and said goodnight, then drove home to try to get some sleep. She was in good hands, and the nursing staff had my cell-phone number if it was needed.

As I drove, I couldn't stop thinking that Jesus is the Alpha and the Omega, that He knows everything and works through time to give us exactly what we need to deal with our moment now.

My mind raced back to the day a few years earlier when I stepped off the bleachers at a Catholic Men's Gathering to introduce myself to someone who had just talked about the importance of men meeting together to grow in their faith. That meeting led me to start a men's fellowship group at my parish, which brought a couple of men who would invite me to an Emmaus retreat just a few months later.

From these seemingly chance situations I was introduced to the verse from Romans 8:28 just weeks before Kristina was diagnosed. My Emmaus brothers gave her a group of true prayer warriors who doctors commented were the reason she survived the ICU months earlier.

I suddenly remembered a small desk plaque Kristina had bought for me a few years earlier while she was on vacation. The plaque read, "Ed, this is God, I will be handling all your problems today so sit back and trust me." I was so overwhelmed that I had to pull over to the side of the highway. I sat there for a few minutes as I cried, thanking God for everything He'd given us.

The next morning when I arrived at the hospital, there was no noticeable change in Kristina. She still didn't have any significant return of memory, but at least physically everything was stable and normal.

The doctor finally visited later that afternoon to summarize the various physician teams' thoughts. She told us that all of Kristina's labs were within normal ranges, though the lupus-related inflammation markers were slightly elevated. They would address that by increasing her steroid dosage for a short period of time. She told us the psychiatry team didn't find anything that stood out to them. They had no reason to continue to keep Kristina at Allegheny General. She explained that we had two options. First, they could transfer Kristina to Western Psych on the other side of town and have her admitted to a psychiatric ward for further evaluation and to help her cope with all the stresses of her illness. Or we could go home. She didn't see any risks to Kristina and thought that over the next few days Kristina would probably regain her memory. The doctor didn't see any reason to move Kristina and recommended we take her home.

I really didn't want to see my daughter admitted to another hospital further away and in a situation where we would have very limited visitation. So, after discussing the options with my wife, we decided that we would take Kristina home and pray that she would recover her memory soon. We set up a follow-up appointment with the psychologist office in the local clinic and were discharged.

On the ride home Kristina then looked at us and said, "Do I know someone named Father Bob?"

"Yes, he's our pastor, Kristina.""

She looked to the side for a moment then turned her eyes back our way and very seriously replied, "I have to talk to him. Jesus wants me to tell him something."

I looked and Connie as she asked Kristina, "What do you need to tell Father Bob? Maybe we can let him know for you."

Kristina quickly responded, "No, Jesus said I have to tell him. This is only for him to hear."

CHAPTER NINETEEN

T he following day at Kristina's urging we called Father Bob and asked if he could come over to see Kristina. We explained nothing more than that she had been in the hospital again over the weekend and would like to see him for a short while. He cheerfully assented, saying that he would come over in the afternoon and bring Holy Communion for Kristina.

When he arrived, we showed him into the living room, where Kristina sat quietly.

As soon as he walked into the room Kristina smiled and said, "Hi, Father Bob."

Connie and I left the room so they could have some time together in quiet without distractions.

It was maybe thirty-minutes later that Father Bob came out of the room and prepared to leave. Connie and I both noticed that his eyes seemed a bit teary and he seemed somewhat distracted.

I shook his hand, showing him to the door, and thanked him for coming over to spend some time with her.

He replied, "It is always a pleasure. I have a lot to think about now because of her."

After he left both Connie and I went to the living room to see Kristina. We really wanted to know if she gave her "message" to Father Bob, but mostly we wanted to know what that message was.

She said they had a very nice talk and she was happy that he brought Jesus to her in the Eucharist. She felt better now.

I asked if she could tell us what the message was now that it had been conveyed to Father Bob.

She looked for a moment and finally replied, "I guess, yes. Jesus only said I had to tell Father Bob first. Now it's OK to tell you. Jesus wanted to tell Father Bob that he is doing a tremendous job in his ministry and that Father Bob in Jesus' opinion is a great shepherd to His flock. Jesus is proud of Father Bob's work."

Connie and I couldn't agree with this message more. Father Bob has always shown himself to be a great shepherd above everything else.

The next morning, I woke early as usual and sat down in my home office to begin the workday. Connie left after breakfast to drive into her office.

A few hours later, Kristina came down the steps outside my office carrying her laptop. She walked into the living room and sat in the recliner, opening her laptop.

A moment later I followed her into the other room. I walked up behind her and asked how she felt. She said she slept well and felt fine. Then I asked the question I really wanted to know the answer to: "Do you remember anything yet?"

She looked up and said she thought that she remembered a few things, just basic things about the house and other innocuous-sounding things. Though these didn't seem dramatic, to me these memories were the greatest news I've heard in a long time.

I told her I was done with my break and had to go back to my office and asked her what she was going to do. She said she was going to look at some things on her laptop. — another thing that excited me, because I hoped just remembering how to use her laptop meant her memory was returning. I smiled and told her I'd be right down the hall if she needed anything.

An hour later I heard her turn the television on, so I took a quick break to check on her. She was sitting in the recliner with her laptop on her lap while she searched the channels for something to watch. I immediately noticed a picture on her laptop, set up as the wallpaper to her main screen. I leaned in to look at the picture more closely. It was a head shot picture of a bearded man with short brown hair and greenish eyes wearing a white robe-like outfit. I asked her what the picture was.

Kristina looked up and said, "That is what Jesus looks like."

I dropped to a knee. "That is what Jesus looks like? Did you see Him?"

"Yes, dad, when we were in the van and in the hospital. He was with me in the ambulance, remember?"

"But, you saw His face and remember what He looks like?"

"Yes, but the picture isn't quite right. His eyes are so beautiful, so much deeper in real life."

I leaned over and worked the mouse to find the title of the picture she had found. Then went back to my office and told my staff that I was going to take an early lunch. I turned on our home computer and put the picture name in the browser:. "The Prince of Peace."

There He was, the man my daughter said was Jesus. My breath was taken away.

At the end of the work day I brought up my personal computer and found the picture myself. I sat in awe looking at the picture. There are so many artistic renditions done through the ages showing Christ's face, but my daughter said this picture was what Jesus really looked like. This was the picture of the man who had come to her in her time of need just 48 hours earlier. "The Prince of Peace— how apt that title was!. Kristina was in turmoil, her memory wiped clean, her fragile health hanging on the edge. And who comes to help her in this dire time? "The Prince of Peace."

I sat looking into the eyes of the man in this picture, something in those eyes brought tears to my eyes. Kristina's words came back to me: "His eyes are so beautiful, so much deeper in real life."

After a few minutes I decided I needed to share this picture with some friends, so I attached the link to an email. In the email I simply wrote, "Check out this link. This is the man Kristina said is Jesus Christ. This is the man who came to her Sunday."

I hit send, then turned back to work.

I got a glass of water from the kitchen and heard my computer notify me of an incoming email, so I quickly turned to see what it was. The email I had just received was a response from a very close friend from Emmaus.

I opened the email and read, "Ed, have you read the book *Heaven Is For Real?*"

Then another email came through: "You need to read *Heaven Is For Real.*"

I responded to both that I hadn't heard of the book before. The first friend called my cell phone within seconds.

He again asked, "You haven't read that book?"

"No."

"Ed, you really need to look that book up online right away. Do it now."

So, since I still had a couple minutes left of my scheduled lunch, I decided to look up this book. I searched, "picture from *Heaven Is For Real*."

The results stunned me. The first hit on the computer was the same exact picture my daughter had found just minutes earlier.

I read a short summary of the book from another site while the picture printed. I grabbed the picture off the printer and went back to Kristina. I asked her if she had ever heard of this book before. She replied that she hadn't. I showed her the picture I had printed from the book.

In the next few hours I received several calls from friends who had seen the picture on the link in my email. Most wanted to know the details of the story about Kristina identifying this picture as the face of Christ. As I related the events of that day, everyone became very excited about this being the face of Christ Himself.

When Connie came home from work that evening, I showed the picture to her as well. We spoke to Kristina about the picture, and she again confirmed she had no doubt that was the man who came to her on Sunday and told her He was Jesus Christ. She told us that the only thing she really remembered from His visit besides what He looked like was that He told her several times to trust Him and that He was there to help her and heal her.

That night, as we prepared for bed, Connie commented that Kristina was feeling none of her normal pain through the evening. I remembered that she hadn't mentioned any pain or discomfort at all throughout the day. Kristina seemed very alert all evening. We also noticed that her memory was getting stronger with each passing hour.

Neither Connie nor I found sleep easy that night as we talked about the picture and remembered that evening almost exactly a year earlier in the emergency room when Kristina had the first visit from the man she knew was Jesus Christ by His voice alone. Now, a year later, she had another visit from Christ—but this time He allowed her to see His face and even told her that He was Jesus Christ. There was no doubt for either of us that He had come to her in her time of need. We couldn't imagine how incredibly blessed we were that Christ had decided to visit our daughter twice

—and in both instances had the same message to give to her: that she needed to trust Him.

How could we ever keep this to ourselves?

The next day passed uneventfully, and again without even a hint of one of Kristina's regular pain or episodes. As the week continued, we knew something miraculous had again occurred for Kristina. This time it seemed that the severe pain and bouts of unconsciousness that had haunted Kristina nightly for the past five months were gone virtually overnight. With that Sunday and this visit from Jesus Christ, all those traumatic episodes ended—and, praise be to God, have never returned to this day.

My wife and I noticed that the readings during Mass each Sunday over the next few weeks seemed to have something that was pertinent to what we'd been through. We found it interesting and exciting that God was using the scriptures to speak to us through Mass. As never before, Christ seemed very present in the readings and in the Mass. We were amazed how the readings seemed to line up perfectly in the Lectionary to fit everything we'd been through in the past weeks.

Even the homilies given by the priests during Mass seemed to be talking directly to us.

Connie spoke to her mom that following Sunday evening. She told her all that had gone on the previous week. She was equally surprised and excited by what had transpired.

The next evening her mother called back to tell us that Connie's father had told one of his friends about what had happened with Kristina. His friend told him that it seemed to him that whatever demon had held onto Kristina was thrown out by Christ. —that maybe the memory loss was due to the demon being pushed out, leaving an emptiness behind.

We hadn't thought about that before, but suddenly so many things made sense. Over that past months we had prayed over Kristina during her most extreme hours of pain because we had noticed the prayers seemed to calm her, even if only slightly. I remembered how, weeks before this memory loss, I had hung blessed medal of St. Benedict the Abbot from her bedpost—the one that was supposed to be a protection from evil.. . . Now we were hearing someone who was completely outside everything that had happened over the past year tell us that it seemed to him that a demon had been forced out of our daughter.

Looking back over the past months, Connie and I had thought many times that there was more to Kristina's screaming episodes than just pain. We commented several times that this seemed much more intense. Connie even mused once about the possibility of some kind of demonic influence. I spent many long nights praying over Kristina with the thought of demonic interaction being involved. This seemed somehow to fit the explanation of Kristina's memory loss and the immediate disappearance of her pain episodes.

CHAPTER TWENTY

The next weeks were happily uneventful. Kristina had no further episodes of either pain or blacking out. Her strength seemed to be returning, and her memory was fully restored. The lab work taken for Kristina's follow-up appointments with her rheumatologist showed steady improvement overall, and especially in her kidney function. It seemed that now the medications were finally really taking control of the lupus and allowing her body to heal. Within a few months, the doctor even remarked that the protein levels in her urine was only slightly elevated.

As a family all we could do was thank God for the miracles. Just a year ago, the doctor had told Kristina she would probably be on medication to help her kidneys remove fluid from her system for the rest of her life. But

now the doctor had that medication nearly
completely removed from her daily regimen:
the little she was taking was mostly as a protective agent for her kidneys, not to help move
fluid from her body.

I spent the next weeks working on the talk
I was soon to give during the April Emmaus
retreat. God was using this preparation to
teach me what trusting Him truly meant. A
few months earlier I had been at a very low
point in my faith. My prayer life was struggling. I had stopped regularly reading my
Bible and was simply existing each day. As
the retreat came closer I could feel a definite
change in my heart. That confession in the
fall in which Father Joe identified a "trust issue with God" in my life started the change,
but this talk was certainly God opening my
eyes to trusting Him more fully then ever by
simply making me study and focus on trust.

April's retreat quickly came. As I did my final preparations in my small room that Saturday evening before my talk, I knew God had
called me out of the darkness in which my
soul had been traveling and now was preparing me to move further than I could ever
imagine. And as I entered the chapel where I

would give this talk, all I could think is how much my faith had changed in just a few weeks. When I originally agreed to give this talk on trust, my choice of entry music was "Be Not Afraid." The song was selected not because I was thinking that we shouldn't be afraid when facing trials: in fact, I had selected this song at the time because I was living in a state of deep fear. Now, as I walked into the room, I could only think how inside my soul was singing "how great is our God." Such a transition within my spirit had taken place.

My talk that night was a summary Kristina's story, told with the emotions that I still to this day feel about the events that had happened over that 13 or 14 months from Kristina's original diagnosis through those days of the second visit she had from Christ. I stood before 50 or so men and watched emotions grow within many of them as the story unfolded. And as I wrapped up the talk I turned a page over to face the men who had been listening for the past hour. On this page was the picture of "The Prince of Peace." Everyone leaned in to get a closer look, and several men gasped when I told them this picture showed Jesus Christ as seen by my daughter Kristina that Sunday in January.

After the talk and other events of the evening finished we stood around the dining area eating a small snack. Terry, one of my new brothers on the retreat, approached me and asked, "Have you read the book, *Heaven Is For Real?*"

I hadn't read the book yet but I told him that I knew the picture was the same one shown in the book. He told me that not long before he had suddenly lost his wife. He didn't know why he had come to the retreat except that he needed something he had heard this retreat offered. For him that was a renewed faith and hope. He told me that when I told my story he was deeply moved and excited to know that Christ was actively moving in our world. He needed to know that after all he had suffered losing his wife. Terry said that when I turned that picture over it brought him to tears. He looked at that picture and knew in his heart that this man was Jesus Christ. The story renewed Terry's hope and gave him back a passion that he even lacked before his wife had died.

The next week Terry texted me and asked if he could join the men's group Saturday at our parish. That Saturday morning Terry showed up at the church holding the book for me to read. He offered it to me as a gift for what was given to him during my talk the week before.

The next day I started to read the book I looked more into the painting done by the young girl of the "Prince of Peace." It took a very short time to finish the book, I was so enthralled. And as I came to the close of the book, I couldn't believe what I was reading as the painter gave her description of Christ. She said, "He's pure, He's very masculine, really strong and big. And His eyes are just beautiful." In the book, *Heaven Is For Real*, little Colton described Jesus similarly, "And His eyes. Oh Dad, His eyes are too pretty." Kristina's words after she had found "The Prince of Peace" painting online rushed back at me, and I fell to my knees in tears. "His eyes are so beautiful, so much deeper in real life."

As I knelt in the room with tears running down my face all I could think is, no matter how talented the artist, how could anyone capture the divine in simple paint? As I sat gazing into those green eyes in the picture before me, I could understand how Peter and the other disciples could leave behind their lives to follow this man after a simple invitation. His eyes must have captured their souls. I knew then that everyone who gazed into the eyes of Christ would see all the depths of His divinity. His eyes captivated my daughter enough that her comments when finding the picture were simply "Yes, that's him. But those eyes!"

CONCLUSION

God does work in strange and incredible ways. The months before Kristina's diagnosis I thought my faith was strong. My family prayed, went to Mass, volunteered in the church and believed in Christ. But in the long 14 months of her worst experiences of this illness we discovered a much deeper faith in Christ than ever imagined.

My "strong" faith was broken in that year. Before Kristina's diagnosis, I had thought my faith was solid. At times over those months I displayed a strength in my faith and actions that uplifted Kristina and others around me. I would pray so often during the day that it seemed at times that all my thoughts were of prayer.

But then, as we moved through the deepest trials, I found myself struggling. Especially in the months after Kristina's desperate days in the ICU I found myself worn out and weak. That first evening in the ICU my faith faltered as I couldn't accept God's word and promises. I was faced with Abraham's choice to give his child to God, but my answer that evening was "no." Then, over the following months, my prayer time lessened and time spent reading the Bible slowly dwindled. I began a slow descent, falling into a dark night within my soul.

But through God's grace and love, He pulled me out of this dark place. He gave me saving guidance through the words of a priest, and then guided events on that Emmaus retreat, inspiring the retreat leader to ask me to talk about my love of God through my trust in Him—a trust he didn't realize had started to fail. I realized that God was guiding me in the preparation for this retreat to study trust when all my trust in Him had failed.

I still sometimes find myself at night holding onto the crucifix repeating those words of faith, "Jesus I trust You." But now I know deep within that, no matter what challenges may come, I will hold onto Jesus and trust in

Him, because I know He is sovereign and very much real.

I now have more faith and trust in God than I ever thought possible. I was asked if I would have been able to keep my faith if things had gone differently in those dark days in the ICU. I know now that I would have really struggled, but in the end would have had nothing but faith in God to hold me through. I am graced with a wife who never wavered in the darkest hours, and through her faith she gave me a light when I was in that darkest night. Her words that night were echoed time after time in scripture, by holy writings of St. Faustina, and by the words of Christ Himself to my daughter: "Trust me."

My prayer is that this story will continue to affect people, opening their hearts to the reality of Christ and the deep love He has for us all. I've seen so many instances of this story drawing people to the edge of their seats and watched as those listening grew in excitement as the story unfolded. I've seen men and women who had completely walked away from their faith do a 180 in their lives, completely changing their ways and giving themselves to Christ.

There is no way that I can ever successfully describe in these pages what truly happened in these events, because there are no words I can come up with that can explain everything that occurred as completely as the experience of being in the moments described.

Jesus said in the Bible, and through many of the saints of the Church, the same message conveyed in those months of severest illness for Kristina: "Don't be afraid. Trust me." Remember always that, when the night seems the darkest, Christ's light and presences shines brightest.

Jesus told St. Faustina to sign another famous painting with the same words.

"Jesus, I trust in You."